CAMERON TAYLOR was born in Orkney and was brought up there and in Aberdeen. He studied History at Aberdeen University then embarked on a career in the UK Civil Service including a two year secondment at 10 Downing Street. He retained strong roots in Orkney and in 1994 was delighted to return home to become Chief Executive of Orkney Tourist Board. In 1999 he went freelance and established Seabridge Consultants, a heritage and tourism consulting business specialising in ancestral tourism developments.

Cameron first became involved in the development of ancestral tourism in Scotland when he co-founded the 1999 Orkney Homecoming, bringing 250 people of Orcadian origin back to their ancestral homeland for a series of emotional reunions. He has been a consultant to Scotland's national AncestralScotland initiative since its inception, is master trainer for an ancestral tourism training course and has written and lectured in Scotland, the US and Canada on various aspects of Scotland's ancestral heritage. Cameron was chairman of the Orkney Homecoming 2007.

His interest in ancestral research has brought friendship and newly discovered kinship with people all round the world.

Rooted in Scotland

Getting to the heart of your Scottish heritage

CAMERON TAYLOR

Luath Press Limited

EDINBURGH

www.luath.co.uk

First Published 2007

ISBN (10): 1-905222-89-0
ISBN (13): 978-1-905222-89-6

The paper used in this book is recyclable. It is made from low
chlorine pulps produced in a low energy, low emission manner from
renewable forests.

Printed and bound by
Bell & Bain Ltd., Glasgow

Typeset in 10.5 point Sabon
by 3btype.com

For Angela, Jamie and Hannah

Acknowledgements

A number of people provided information, advice, encouragement and inspiration during the research and writing of this book. Particular thanks are due to:

Ewan Colville, VisitScotland
George Taylor Eunson
Violet Eunson
David Forsyth, National Museum Scotland
Alison Fraser, Orkney Library and Archive
Kevin Halliwell, National Library of Scotland
Max Johnson, The Great Canadian Travel Company
Brian Lambkin and Patrick Fitzgerald, Centre for Migration Studies
May McInnes
Ann McVeigh, Public Record Office of Northern Ireland
Joanna O'Rourke, National Archives of Scotland
George Patton, Ulster Scots Agency
Tony Reid, Scottish Roots
William Roulston, Ulster Historical Foundation
Angela Taylor
Russell Walker, Scottish Executive
Carl Watt, Scottish Museums Council

It goes without saying that responsibility for any errors or omissions rests with me. Please let me know of any corrections or suggested additions via our web site www.rootedinscotland.com

Cameron Taylor

Contents

CHAPTER I

Home is Where the Heart is

A Homecoming

MAY 1999: We are waiting for the arrival of a ferry at the ancient harbour of Stromness in the Orkney Islands, lying just six miles off the north coast of the Scottish mainland. Two hundred and fifty North Americans are about to arrive in order to take part in a homecoming celebration, the culmination of years of planning and preparation. It is a still, calm evening – not a breath of wind, and gone are the spring showers that had fallen earlier: a perfect end to the day. As the ferry manoeuvres towards the jetty we hear the skipper's announcement: 'Ladies and gentlemen, we are now approaching Stromness. The harbour front you see is essentially unchanged since your ancestors left these islands, so ladies and gentlemen, welcome home.' There was not a dry eye on board the ferry, or amongst those of us waiting on shore. It was an intensely emotional moment, one that I am sure neither the Homecomers nor the local Orcadians will ever forget.

The Homecomers stayed in Orkney for a week, during which time they explored their ancestry, discovered the locations of now-abandoned crofts – once hearth and home but now no more than tumbled heaps of stones surrounded by fields and heather – and joined the people of Orkney for a gala evening, a celebration of kinship and shared connections. Meeting the Homecomers, listening to their stories and sharing in the emotions they were experiencing as a result of their visit, convinced me of the profound importance of our sense of rootedness and belonging.

The Sense of Connection

Do you feel rooted too, somehow, by the knowledge of an ancestral connection with Scotland? Many of Scotland's other sons and daughters, including those spread across the world in a huge diaspora, do too. That sense of connection – an awareness of the significance of your ancestry – is an important and powerful force, and is often a very emotional one, though it need never be a source of embarrassment.

Scotland's worldwide diaspora has created connections between this small country and virtually every part of the globe. The connections are the ties of family, shared experience and of common cultural heritage. Emigration and the nature of Scotland's diaspora experience have been studied, analysed, made the subject of learned books and articles. At an intellectual level we can study the emigration phenomenon, aiming to understand the reasons for it, the nature of the experience and its consequences. Genealogists will piece together family trees, skeletons of past lives. Family historians will take one perspective; social and economic historians, others. But for many ordinary people the defining moment in their journey of discovery is an emotional one: quite literally, when they begin walking in their ancestors' footsteps.

In *Rooted in Scotland*, we will explore the various ways in which you may begin tracing your family history, or continuing the search if you have already made a start on piecing together your family tree. With the growth of the Internet, it is increasingly easy to do genealogical research from across the globe, and we examine the best sources by which you can do so from the comfort of your own home or office, wherever that may be.

You may live in the US or Canada, New Zealand, Australia or anywhere in the world. Even closer to home, you may be in England or perhaps in Scotland itself. Wherever you are, your Scottish ancestry is worth exploring and celebrating. This book will help you do both. In later chapters we will examine some of the ways in which you can embark on your own journey of exploration, but for now let us begin with three fundamentals of any life, and therefore, any family tree: birth, marriage and death.

A Death in the Family

In constructing family trees – skeletons of the past – it is easy to lose sight of one simple fact: these names and dates on paper refer to real people who once lived and loved, perhaps sharing the same hopes and fears, dreams and desires, as you and I. I was reminded of this recently at my auntie's funeral. An elderly woman, she passed away after a short but difficult illness. While her death was no surprise to the family, it affected everyone nonetheless. As a fairly typical family, we are not very close, but we are brought together by death, marriage and the birth of children – the punctuation marks in the story of every family.

My cousin asked me to help with the arrangements at the funeral – in other words, to join him and the other dark-suited, sombre men (and one woman) of the closest family and friends in the sad duty of carrying the coffin. I hope my cousin will forgive me for writing about his mother's funeral, but it is important to reflect on what happened and how it affects our attitude to ancestral research.

A funeral is a ritual, of course, designed to ease gently, with dignity, the separation of the deceased from their family and friends. As we took our places in the church, the significance of what we were involved in struck home. Addressing the mourners, the minister said that my auntie had been baptised in the same church in 1919 and it was her wish, clearly expressed in the last days of her life, that her funeral service take place in the same church. She must have felt – rightly so – that doing so was an appropriate way of closing the circle of her long life. The minister went on to tell us that she had also chosen the two hymns for the funeral service; each meant something special to her and were part of how she wanted to be remembered.

At the end of the short service, we carried her coffin out of the church, past the hundred or so people who had joined us for the funeral service. Most heads were bowed and few people watched us as we carried the coffin out of the church; fewer still made eye contact. But for those few minutes, everyone there was connected in a very real, immediate way. At the graveyard the last rites were performed and we lowered my auntie's coffin into her grave. The headstone there already bore the name of my uncle, who died more than 20 years previously, and on it my auntie's name will now join his.

I do not wish to be maudlin – my point in reflecting on this is that, a hundred years from now, when a future generation of ancestral researchers do their work, they will find merely the record of my auntie's death and a time-worn headstone. Tangible records will tell only a tiny, tiny part of the story. We need to bear that in mind in doing our own research, today.

Marriage: The Dance of the Families

In complete contrast to funerals, however, there is marriage, an act that binds together two people but which also, significantly, brings together two families.

My brother-in-law got married recently, and the wedding took place in the historic Borders town of Melrose, in a beautiful National Trust for Scotland house. We all gathered there the night before the wedding, and staying in the same house, members of the two families were all able to spend quite a bit of time together. The families had not, on the whole, met before and there began a subtle, complex series of social manoeuvres as people sized each other up.

In this dance of the families, common ground was sought: areas of difference identified, potential alliances born, husbands, wives and children discussed. It was all very polite, but ultimately very, very serious. I suppose, deep down, this was survival of the species on a social scale – each family, a tribe with its own rituals and traditions, was determining whether the other would help or hinder its survival.

Did I read too much into this? I do not think so. I wondered whether the marriage ceremony would be a catalyst in bringing people together. Of course, the bride and groom, visibly and wholeheartedly in love, were by now very much together and already the proud parents of a baby daughter, Rose. The marriage was a civil ceremony and the officiating Registrar did her best to give everyone present a sense of being part of something special. After the wedding we drank champagne, families mingling in the happy afterglow of a successful ceremony, and continued on to the reception. In his after-dinner speech, my brother-in-law, normally quiet and rather reserved, shocked everyone by eloquently declaring his love for his wife and child, prompting an enthusiastic toast, the first of many.

Baby Rose, of course, was oblivious to all this emotion. The dance of the families will not even be part of her early memories. To her, 'family' will mean parents, grandparents and maybe even great-grandparents and a coterie of uncles, aunties and cousins, some she will feel close to, but others she will see only on rare yet significant occasions – births, marriages and deaths: the cycle of ceremonies begun again.

New Beginnings: Birth

The birth of a child is a wonderful thing. Twenty-one years ago, when our son was born, I was there to witness the everyday miracle of childbirth that midwives take in their stride, but which was, for my wife and I, a life-changing experience. For my wife, of course, the birth was physically and emotionally draining: there are times when it is good to be a man, and this was surely one of them! A couple of days after his birth, I went to the local registry office to record my son's details. It felt like a rite of passage, a ceremony marking an important stage in all of our lives. I dutifully gave the information the Registrar requested and the official record of James Cameron Taylor's arrival was created. Future generations of researchers will find a wealth of information in the records, though I must admit to making a mistake when recording my wife's place of birth. I know we should have had the record corrected by now, but there is part of me that doesn't want to make it *too* easy for future researchers.

In fact, ancestral researchers will have a bit of bother with me in any case. Although I was born in Scotland, my wife is English and we were married in Yorkshire. Our son was born in London, before we moved to Scotland, where our daughter was then born. So, lots of work for future researchers to do to track us down, create a family tree and then flesh that out with more personal information which transforms a family tree into true family history.

On the registration of births, the official Register records only the facts of the event and sufficient information to link it to other events. It doesn't record my sense of pride in becoming father to a son, or the good wishes of family and friends on the occasion of the birth. It captures none of the emotion surrounding the event.

I return to the mention made of my brother-in-law's wedding earlier. After the wedding ceremony was complete, a very moving naming ceremony for baby Rose took place. It was the first time I'd witnessed such an event. My brother-in-law and his wife had decided to leave Rose to make her own decision about baptism when she was old enough to do so, but they did want to mark her birth in a special way. So the Registrar who had conducted the wedding ceremony led the naming proceedings, inviting in turn Rose's auntie, a family friend and her grandmother to say a few words about their hopes and aspirations for Rose and each made a commitment to support and encourage her in her journey through life.

The formal record of Rose's birth will not convey the sense of emotion present during the ceremony, or of how, for example, the speechmakers managed to cope with the emotion of the moment. But we are lucky in the era in which we live: researchers in the future will have access to photographs and video footage capturing in candid – sometimes embarrassingly so – detail a record of the event. Consider how precious photographs of our ancestors are to us. Surely we have an obligation on us, today, to leave a similarly tangible record of our lives for the benefit of our descendants.

Where is Everyone?

After the records of births, marriages and deaths, the next most useful source of information for ancestral researchers – in Scotland as well as elsewhere – is the ten-yearly census. In Scotland, a comprehensive census has been undertaken every ten years since 1841 (except 1941), providing a rich, detailed record of every household in the country. The census is a wonderful resource for researchers and genealogists, and we will consider it in detail later: for now, however, I would like to share my own experience of collecting information for the 1981 census.

At the time, my wife – then a civil servant – was involved in helping collect census returns from a single street in London. I helped as best I could; it was just one street but it seemed the most enormous of tasks and certainly put the magnitude of the whole exercise into perspective. We had to identify each individual household, make sure they got the forms to fill in, and then collected the completed forms after census night. Some people completed the forms willingly and were easy to contact in order to collect the forms; others were difficult or impossible to contact. A few simply refused to take part in the census at all. Multiply our experience from that one street into whole towns and cities, and just think about the persistence required by the small army of people who are charged with getting the census completed. We should not take the use of our wonderful, historic census resources for granted.

The Idea of Home

The word 'home' means different things to different people, and for some it can mean several things all at the same time. 'Home' can mean the place we were born, in other words, our first home, or the place where we grew up, that spot on the map and in the heart from whence our childhood memories stem. For others, 'home' can mean simply the place they currently live. Married couples, after all, often talk of 'setting up home' together in terms of making a new beginning. At another level, the idea of home can be associated with the notion of an ancestral homeland, a place where something greater than any one individual began. It is easy to underestimate just how powerful an experience visiting an ancestral homeland can be, enabling you to touch the past in a very real, very personal way.

The title of this chapter is intended to echo this important sense of home as a place connected with family origins and strong emotions. Such an ancestral 'home' may be far away from your current home, but the feeling of connection is no less strong despite the distance. The idea of homeland is the stuff of the heart, not just the head. Sceptics may raise their eyebrows at this, but thousands of people all over the world spend time, energy and money identifying and then visiting their ancestral homelands. To them, the idea of home and homeland is very real, and we should not – indeed cannot – underestimate the importance of this.

Rooted in Scotland

We have set the scene for the journey of homecoming we will embark on together, using this book as a guide. We have reflected on the idea of home and seen the importance of a return to an ancestral homeland. We have explored the reality of death, marriage and birth, those punctuation marks in a family's history that are recorded in the official records we find so useful as ancestral researchers. We have considered the census too, an enormous undertaking that provides us with a wealth of information as genealogists. Our journey through the rest of *Rooted in Scotland* begins with the experiences of Scotland's emigrants as they travelled across the world. Our heroes and heroines are not the glamorous, unreachable actors in Hollywood movies, but are ordinary people like you and I, whose lives we can read as stories of which we too are part. Our journey of heritage is one of celebration, not just of discovery, and we will find much of which to be proud. The journey is also one of exploration and we will find that underlying all the research, the documents and connections is the simple truth that you must touch your past in order to know it.

There is a wealth of information available to help you understand these stories, and our journey together will introduce you to some of the most useful sources. These routes to your roots can sometimes become tangled and difficult to negotiate, so we will look for assistance along the way.

Reaching your ancestral homeland is part of the journey. It is a physical act, making manifest the sense of connection in your head and in your heart. Visiting your homeland is not the end of the journey, though; it may only be the beginning. Indeed, you may choose to return and revisit again and again.

CHAPTER 2

To Cross the Broad Atlantic

ONE OF THE PRINCIPAL THEMES of this book is that of journeys: the journey of each of us through our own life, the journey of a family from its origins to the present generation, and the genealogical journey through research and eventual return to visit the ancestral homeland in Scotland.

One journey, however, is perhaps most significant in any family history: the emigration journey, that transition from one world to another during which people simply sought to endure, to reach their destination alive and, on arrival, re-establish a home for themselves and their loved ones. Emigration is a defining moment in any family history. Even the language used to describe this implies a transition of sorts. People *emigrate* from Scotland, but when they arrived at their destination they were *immigrants*. They were no longer leaving a place, they were arriving at one. Between departure and arrival was the arduous journey itself.

The focus of this chapter is the time of transition between departing and arriving. Insight into this journey will help you understand the humanity of your family history and your sense of rootedness.

The Emigration Experience

Even for people who looked upon their emigration as an opportunity and their journey as an adventure, the moment of departure from Scotland must have been almost too much to bear. To leave the place you had been born and grown up and set off into the relative unknown, often in uncomfortable conditions in a fragile wooden (or later metal) ship, to say your farewells knowing that, in all likelihood, you would never again see the people who stayed behind... it is hard for us to imagine the finality of such a departure. Today, we send text messages and emails as we travel. We can speak to each other on the telephone and instantly get news of events at home via our conversations or over the Internet. Using videoconferencing and web cams, we can even see each other over distances of thousands of miles. Our ancestors lived in almost unimaginably different times.

Migration within Britain itself was certainly more straight-forward than emigration overseas. As the Agricultural Revolution changed land management practices and the Industrial Revolution created a seemingly endless need for labour, people were encour-aged – sometimes forced – to move within Scotland and from Scotland to England to fill shortages in local labour markets. These domestic migrations are not as well-documented as the overseas migrations, apart from the much-discussed Highland Clearances, and do not appear to be nearly so traumatic as were the interna-tional emigrations.

Countless letters and diaries exist to document overseas migration journeys. Indeed, we are fortunate that recording their experiences were popular ways in which people coped with the boredom of long sea voyages. These letters and diaries or journals survive today in private hands and in archives and libraries. The National Library of Scotland (www.nls.uk) has a particularly fine collection of documents, including propaganda-filled Emigrants' Guides designed to persuade people to emigrate and advise them in doing so.

Care must be taken, however, when using sources of information such as letters, diaries and guides. We may have only one side of letter-based correspondence, for example, and letter-writers may not have told the whole truth, avoiding mention of dangerous experiences and hoping thereby to avoid alarming their friends and relatives who remained at home. Diaries, on the other hand, were generally written as private documents and therefore give a more honest personal account – yet there is always the risk that they too might have been intended as guides for others and may emphasise successes rather than failures. Emigrant Guides almost certainly emphasised the positive aspects of emigration at the expense of the negative, and therefore do not give the full story. None of this is to say that we should reject such sources of information; we simply need to read between the lines and to use them carefully.

I would like to introduce you to two accounts of emigration journeys. The first was written for publication by Robert Louis Stevenson, one of Scotland's best known novelists. The second is a first-hand emigration diary written by my own grandfather, Sutherland Simpson Taylor. Although a personal account, his diary does seem to have been intended for a wider readership. It is included here in full as an example of one migrant's personal account of his journey, which also reflects a universal experience.

Robert Louis Stevenson

Born in Edinburgh in 1850, Robert Louis Stevenson was a prolific novelist, poet and travel writer. In 1879–80 he travelled across the Atlantic to New York by steamship and then onwards to California by train, illustrating a point that we sometimes forget: emigrants didn't just complete the sea journey and disembark from the ship with – no doubt – a profound sense of relief and then stop. Most continued their journeys onwards into North America, into the big eastern cities or across the western plains; their onward journeys after arrival also took weeks to complete.

For Stevenson's travels, he chose to cross the Atlantic in steerage class in order to see how 'ordinary' people travelled. Although in the event he was persuaded by friends to buy a better class of ticket, he still spent most of his time in steerage and wrote a fascinating account of his experiences, *The Amateur Emigrant,* which was written during the journey but was not published in full until 1895. Middle-class Victorian society found the book shocking in its descriptions of the conditions endured in steerage class.

Upon arriving in New York, Stevenson continued his journey to California by train, once again documenting his experiences in *Across the Plains*, which was published in 1892.

Reading these two books will give you an excellent insight into an emigration journey of the late 19th century. You can read or download *The Amateur Emigrant* and *Across the Plains* online, free, courtesy of the University of Adelaide library in its e-books collection, available at http://etext.library.adelaide.edu.au/. Bear in mind as you read that the journey would have been considerably more difficult in earlier times. Sailing across the Atlantic, for example, took much longer than making the journey by steamship, though neither journey could have been particularly comfortable. Before the railroads were built, people had to travel across the continent on horseback, by wagon, or on foot.

Like an estimated 25 per cent of emigrants, Stevenson returned to Scotland. There were many different reasons for return journeys of this sort. Some migration was of a temporary economic nature, such as the contract-based work that took so many Scots to work in Canada for the Hudson's Bay Company. Some migrants simply didn't succeed in establishing themselves in the new country and returned home, while illness or bereavement was also cause for a return home. We shouldn't think that the flow of people was entirely, nor permanently, one way.

Sutherland Simpson Taylor's Emigration Diary

Sutherland Simpson Taylor was born in Orkney in 1877, son of George and Johana Taylor. George was a farmer and fisherman and Sutherland would have been destined for the same life, but in 1907, aged 29, he decided to emigrate to North America.

Sutherland kept a diary in the form of a small notebook, written in pencil. The diary records the details of his journey up until he arrives at his eventual destination. It is included in full here, with minimal editing, so that Sutherland tells his story in his own words. I have included some comments as footnotes.

Thanks go to George Eunson for transcribing the diary and to

May MacInnes for allowing its publication. Here is Sutherland's story.

Getting all things arranged. We[1] took 1.05 p.m. train for Edinburgh[2] making a more speedy journey than first mentioned. On getting to Old Edinburgh we made ourselves more at home again, meeting many of our old friends[3] and spending a most enjoyable time, but as in all other places the time for parting came, making the last in Bonny Scotland of the many known and kind friends.

Glasgow again being reached Tuesday evening, and having a very few calls to make we made to our temporary home which is so-called lodgings, having a good night's sleep in a finely well suited room near to where the steamer sailed from.

We found our way to the last place for embarkation about 8.00 a.m. and on the chap of 9.00 a.m. the signal for starting was again given. Down through the Clyde the *Sarmatian*[4] was guided and steered by tug. The scenery was magnificent, the great ship building yards marvellous, not forgetting to mention the many large steamboats going in and out.

When off Gourock the tug was put ashore for any passengers missed at Glasgow. A few more boarded the steamer to join the happy crowd. Getting under way we resumed our journey down the Clyde taking a few hours to do so, among as mentioned before marvellous wonders of what man can do[5].

---

[1] Sutherland does not record to whom 'we' refers, but the implication is that he was travelling with at least one friend or relative. Passenger lists suggest he may have travelled with James Simpson.

[2] It is not clear precisely when the journey started, or where the train journey began.

[3] We should not think of places like Orkney as remote at this time. People moved around for a variety of reasons and bonds of friendship and family were strong. People relied on friends and relatives for assistance.

[4] The *SS Sarmatian*, built in 1871.

[5] Industrial Glasgow clearly impressed the young Sutherland.

Now we are clear of the Clyde and moving slowly for the next place of call Moville, and as we go across the Irish Sea good weather favours us and spirits good, having now made many new acquaintances. But before crossing I miss to say we pass what is called Elsie [*sic*: Ailsa] Craig, a small mountain plainly speaking, planted in the middle of the ocean about a mile from the Irish coast. Now let us pass on to our new acquaintances of true Scots which you can always speak to so assuredly. We have on board speaking roughly, about 600 emigrants. Out of that number 100 or so are foreigners. Fortunately, they are kept by themselves[6].

Now the night is at hand, supper being served, we find ourselves in bed getting a fair night's rest. We wake up to find ourselves arrived at Moville, a beautiful little village situated on the coast of Ireland. Magnificent to look on all the small crofters houses, passes a few hours. And on shipping over 100 more passengers on board, the signal once more given, we leave passing along the coast viewing all the most interesting scenery. A splendid night prevailed and the most pleasure found in walking the deck. Sleep taking advantage, we found our way to our resting place again for the night, and on getting up next morning found ourselves in Galloway [sic: Galway], a town at almost the most westerly point in Ireland. And on spending most part of the day there and taking on board by another tug boat about 200 more passengers, making the total now between 900–1,000, far in excess of what ought to be, as the accommodations are rather a moderate style. However, we spent a rather good time of it in Galway as we got dancing started, and kept up during the day[7]. Dinner served, we were ready to make

---

[6] It isn't clear why Sutherland is so suspicious of 'foreigners'. It may simply have been because of the language difference. These would have been European migrants in transit to North America.

[7] Dancing was a very popular pastime on board throughout the journey, whenever the weather was not too bad. It kept people entertained and physically active.

another start on our long journey. Once outside we found that most of our company soon found their way to their beds, as the wind and sea was getting rather rough and sickness overtaking them, they were glad to be in their resting place but owing to having few beds some had to sleep on the tables all night[8].

A few hours passed and the weather getting worse, few were seen moving around. Even some of the stewards found it impossible to keep away sea sickness. Fortunately I kept up myself and spent a fair time only. Not an extremely happy time. As the day seems to be drawing on the weather seems nothing improved. It's now breakfast time but out of over 900 people, one tenth of that number has not assembled for any meat. Some of our lady friends are exceptionally bad with sickness. The day passes off quietly, nothing of any kind of amusement to while away time. Tea hour arrives with few to partake of meat. And so passes the evening in a sing-song way until 10.00 p.m., and those who remained on deck got orders to get to bed. On getting to bed the night passes away[9].

As breakfast bell rings we find a few more assembled at the tables. The weather being greatly improved and this being Sabbath day, we passed rather a dull forenoon below owing to the weather, spent rather like a Saturday night in a public house than a Sunday, drink being freely served out to those who take it, the charge being 6d a pint. A very uproarious night was passed, only it passed away the time to watch and listen to the many arguments among the different classes of people. This went on until the bell rang to clear away everyone to his own room. This we do and partake of what sleep we can catch. However this night passes again.

---

[8] Overcrowding of this sort was common and must have made the journey especially tedious, particular if fellow passengers were suffering from sea-sickness. Seasickness is a common theme in diaries of this sort.

[9] Already at this early stage of the voyage, routine is setting in.

Breakfast bell rings again and few partake of food as the weather has got a great deal worse, and as the day glides away slowly and the weather gets even worse, we find little enjoyment on deck and much less below[10]. However, a few of us make the time pass a little better by card playing, but we soon get wearied and tired and sometimes on deck, other times below, we pass away the forenoon. It's now dinner hour but few again are at the dinner tables, some not being able to leave their beds, while a greater number are to be seen lying about the deck. It's now pretty rough and rather an awkward cross-swell. As the day passes on and the only amusement is found in card playing and telling stories and so, on goes the afternoon and tea-time arrives once more is served, and taken, we assemble all together and mix. A most enjoyable evening was spent [as] we have had as yet and carried on until ten, that being the appropriate time to retire. Little sleep was found for sometime owing to heavy weather, which lashed for four hours making it impossible for the *Sarmatian* to make any headway at all.

Fortunately it eases off as the morning draws on, but still very rough. Today, Wednesday, has passed quietly, but a concert is arranged for this evening[11]. Tea served as usual, the concert starts at 8.00 p.m. and kept up till 10.30 p.m.

Thursday being a better morning, much more pleasure was found on deck but the afternoon was foggy and very slow rate of speed was made. Luckily it cleared off and we had the pleasure of looking on a large iceberg, almost about ¼ mile distance away, it being a sight few if any on board had seen before. The weather is considerably better

---

[10] This is an uncomfortable time for the passengers, with so much sea-sickness. Weather conditions had a major impact on any transatlantic voyage. How much worse it must have been before the days of steamships and for people making the even longer journey to Australia or New Zealand.

[11] Organised concerts gave the participants something to occupy their time and the audience something to look forward to.

now and as the sun sets red in the northwest it appears very beautiful. Our usual concert takes place tonight again and passes off a pleasant pastime.

We go to sleep again and wake up to find a beautiful morning which all hands take advantage. Sports are carried out to a great extent. Tug-of-war teams now pull, also a game they call 'kites' and then dancing is carried on the deck and again the concert at night[12]. We now sight a full rigged sloop in the Banks of Newfoundland. It is said we are not far from another iceberg and the air is very much colder. Today we have little or no sport, but we expect to engage in some for the afternoon and night.

Forgot to mention yesterday at the tug-of-war the Scotch were set against the Irish and the foreigners was to tackle the winners, but owing to a dispute which arose between the Scotch and Irish of whom won, it was not carried out.

It is now Saturday afternoon and a thick fog prevails and if keeps thick I fear we won't reach Boston as thought on Monday[13]. Dancing is going on briefly on deck at present and will continue till dark. Now as I have written up to the present everything which has passed I may say a word on how we are fed. We get porridge every morning and meatloaf, cold meat or cottage pie, ham and egg. Dinner, we get soup, potatoes and meat, usually a different kind and finish off with dessert of say rice and rhubarb or pudding. Tea, we get bread and butter, or at least called butter, and marmalade and corned beef. Then we get gruel at 7.30 p.m. to finish up with[14].

---

[12] This was a busy day, with everyone trying to pack as much exercise and activity into the time between poor weather conditions.

[13] Frustration about a delayed arrival must have been difficult to bear, especially for people who had been suffering from seasickness during the journey.

[14] Food seems to have been plentiful on board the *Sarmatian*, but Sutherland's remark about the butter suggests that it may not have been of the best quality, especially towards the end of the voyage.

Now I've given you full details of meat, so I shall pass on to where I left off. Am going to sleep.

We again wake up to find a very cold morning. We have a secret meeting[15] at 10.00 in the morning and again at 6.00 p.m. The Irish are singing and dancing, and the foreigners[16]. They are at all sorts of fun. Sunday passed.

We go on to Monday, a better day for good weather and meat. The day advances. We sight about half a dozen fishing boats lying away out to sea, between 200 or 300 miles from land and at the time of writing, I now look on a three-masted ship homeward bound. It's now almost tea-time and later on a concert is to be held in the second cabin on behalf of the widows and orphans[17]. Tickets 6d each and it will be the last on board ship. And now the time has passed. I expect there won't be many sorry hearts on board when we sight land, which we are expected to do by our arrival on 7 May, making the long journey of 14 days[18].

We are now reaching our destination at 8.00 a.m. at last and we are nearing Boston. Have seen many a wonderful sight, far too numerous to mention. Places I have seen what I consider a life sight with regards to large ships and of coming up the bay. The scenery was lovely. Many sorry hearts were on board as we partook of our last breakfast on board the *Sarmatian*·[19]

---

[15] It is not clear what this 'secret meeting' is about, or who is involved. It may be a meeting of Masons as there is some evidence that Freemasons looked after each other's interests during emigration voyages and on arrival.

[16] Relations between the Scots, Irish and foreigners were clearly much improved by the end of the voyage.

[17] Typically, such concerts were organised by the better-off emigrants occupying the more comfortable accommodation on board.

[18] Sutherland expresses relief at having arrived but compared with some other journeys, especially pre-steamship ones, this was not a long passage.

[19] The expression of regret here is probably about parting from friends, not about the end of the sea journey.

We glided slowly up to our berth guided by the tug until we reached our last landing place. We had a great deal of trouble to get cleared out. We had to wait a considerable time on board before we were permitted ashore, and after we got our feet on land, once more we felt a little more lifted up, but owing to having many different formalities to go through, it took a considerable long time to get through it all. We just had to pass the doctor after that, show vaccination card, show your money and asked so many numerous questions, that it would take a much longer time and space to tell it than what I could afford[20]. I also may say we also had to get our railway ticket and money changed, also boxes and hand bags overhauled by customs authorities and all this goes on in a large shed belonging to The Allan Line Company.

We spent 6 hours in that shed before we got clear, then we got a tram to take us to the main station in Boston. On arriving at the station we had a little transaction to go through, but on getting finished we went to look for a little dinner, and on getting that we went to do a little shopping. I mean a few provisions for our journey from Boston to Seattle. I saw but little of Boston as we had just 1½ hours to spare, but what I did see of it, it looked very well, mostly wooden houses and very classy shops and business seemed good. Our time for leaving was four o'clock, and on that time arriving we found our way to our train.

We are now on our train journey and so far as I've seen the country looks very beautiful, the fields look lovely and green. The plantations are very pretty as we pass them by.

The accommodations on the train are even worse than that on ship[21]. We don't even have any beds or any other place to

---

[20] The relief and excitement of arrival quickly turns to frustration with all the formalities. Emigration was no longer a simple, informal process.

[21] Train journeys were notoriously uncomfortable.

bed down to have a rest. It's all seats for two and very close together making it impossible to get comfort. This is our second night without any sleep.

We are now in Buffalo. This train is very slow, and stops at many stations. I don't find trains the same as what I thought. There is no stove in carriages as said, so we cannot get a drop of tea made when one has it. I had a cup of tea this morning for breakfast and some bread and butter in the dining salon, but one has got to pay for it there. It may be better on leaving Chicago; we have got to change there. I missed to say that 52 of the passengers on board the *Sarmatian* were returned home again, not being able to pass the doctor.

We pass on our way many towns, one in particular I take much notice of its entire beauty. I also notice in it an exhibition. The name of the place is Euclid Avenue. We are on our way, scores of towns and villages far too numerous to mention.

We have now reached Chicago 10.00 p.m. Wednesday, 8th. We are sent into the beautiful waiting room of Central Station in Chicago, as the first train we could get was 2.43 a.m. We had a little lunch[22] and a small walk through one of the streets. We were very sleepy and tired after being two nights without sleep.

We are now away from Chicago now making our way through more hilly country, many beautiful sights are to be seen, but owing to being very tired and rather worn out, we cannot enjoy the trip very well. I may say there are no beds in any of the trains, nothing but a seat which one could not sleep on with any comfort, and to make matters worse, there is no fire on any train so you can get a drop of tea[23].

---

[22] Presumably he means a light meal rather than lunch.

[23] Sutherland is distinctly unimpressed with the lack of comfort on the trains. You can almost feel his tiredness as he writes.

We have had 2 cups of tea since we left Boston and I may say I have not had 6 cups of tea since I left home.

We are now in a place called Alberta. We had an hour to spare so we went to try and get a good cup of tea. We were very disappointed indeed when what they call green tea was served, but which could not be very much relished.

We have again made a start on our journey which by no means can come too soon. We have now arrived in St Pauls having to change trains again, but to our great disappointment on arrival, we were told we could not get away until 3.00 o'clock Friday afternoon. We got into St Pauls 7.30 p.m. on Thursday. We were sent to a hotel whose proprietors were Swedes, I think. However, we were all very tired and I can assure you we all slept very sound. We paid 25¢ for bed and 5¢ for supper and 3¢ for breakfast, fortunately not as much as thought.

We got away 10.30 a.m. on Friday morning, we're now on our way to Seattle and during our journey we have seen many beautiful and marvellous sights[24]. I missed to say we are travelling in company with a lady and gent belonging to Garbity in Morayshire whose names are James and Mary Newlands, the very best of company whom we have very much indeed enjoyed each other's company. I may say in all confidence anyone leaving home will find the journey not as told by some. You have to do and go through a bit of hardship and a great deal of knocking about before one reaches their destination, but one can still enjoy the trip as long as they are blessed with good health[25].

We have yet 1,600 miles to go and what we can see of that, as far as the eye can reach, it's a very level country and farming is going on apace. We go through prairie and woods

---

[24] A decent night's sleep seems to have lifted Sutherland's spirits and he is again able to appreciate the view.

[25] In other words, don't believe everything you read in the Emigrant Guides!

towns and villages, fruit fields etc. What looks most change is all the houses are wood and as we pass, farming is altogether different. You can see as high as eight horses in one plough and as we go further west, it is all mules instead of horses.

We are now in the state of Minnesota and it does not look very much like summer as the snow lies a depth among the trees. Now since I left off writing we have covered a space of about 400 miles and most of that has been nothing to be seen for miles around but prairie i.e. nothing to be seen but cattle and horses and lots of Indian huts for herding purposes.

As we get along, the country gets more broken and hilly. I may say that from the start of our journey we have got along very well. Only this morning 11 May, our lady friend whom we have had great respect for during the journey got her purse stolen and all the money she had, three five-dollar bills and some small change. The conductor of train went round all the passengers, but all for no good. We feel very sorry for the girl in a foreign land without a home and worst of all without any money[26]. But we shall stick together; by no means shall she want as long as I can help her. Had she been any other than a true, honest, upright girl I should not have done so, but she being one of Scotland's truly tenderest-hearted girls we could not, who belongs to the old country[27], let her go without money. She does not go as far as us by 165 miles.

We have now made as far as a place called Glasgow having telegraphed to our friend in Seattle that we are due there by 7.45 p.m. tomorrow, Sunday. We still continue our journey, this part of the country being very wet and plenty

---

[26] Theft of this sort must have been heart-breaking for the victims, but was probably fairly common.

[27] Here, Sutherland expresses his own feelings of rootedness and connection with a homeland he has only recently left.

of snow and nothing but uncultivated land to be seen as far as the eye can reach and animals lying dead by the score.

We have now made our way as far as the Rocky Mountains which is the one great sight of all sights. We went right through them. It took a great many hours winding to and fro to get through. One time we were looking two or three thousand feet down and the next moment were nothing but mountains looking up. Every hill and dale was a mass of trees all as straight as if made of logs. We rather enjoyed the journey through the mountains, only night coming on we had to give up gazing so we cannot enjoy the journey so well. As one would think being so long in knocking about, for want of sleep cuts ones enjoyment.

We wake up next morning early and the time passes slowly. We can always see a little new to make the trip cheery. Our small misfortune which happened yesterday to our young lady companion getting her money stolen rather made matters a little more disappointing for some time, but as with all other troubles you must forget about it. But I'm proud to say she did not go away without money.

We have now arrived at Wenatchee where our two friends must leave us, being very sorry to part. But a true saying 'the best of friends must part'.

So we are now left all alone for 165 miles more. On leaving Wenatchee we admire the beautiful Cascade Mountains as the train runs along the foot of the mountains between the high mountains and the Columbia River. We follow it along side of it for miles, a more magnificent and more beautiful sight one never looked on, to see the water coming forcing it's [sic] way down the river in a fierce, foaming torrent. One could throw a stone to the other side of the river and trees all sizes coming swirling down and eddying into some creek or corner. Where we are now, it is one mass of tremendous trees of all kinds and diversification.

We spent 7½ hours to get over the mountains and during that time we have had hundreds of turns and even went right through the middle of some of them. One time looking up some thousand feet, other times looking down some thousand feet, seeing nothing during these hours but trees and one mountain or another. It's good we are now on more level country having only now 48 miles to go out of 3,000 or more, the end of what cannot come too soon. One cannot tell the distance from Flotta[28] to Seattle, except those to have gone through the mill.

I trust those who may have the pleasure of reading this will believe me that this is only a small narrative of what has been seen and passed since we left the Old Country. But when one is well and strong they can manage to pull through not so bad. Anyone who is not that, it would be as well to stay at home. Darkness is now at hand and we wait the call out of Seattle which we got at 10.15p.m. Sunday 12th.

As we entered the station we gazed at many faces for a friend to meet us, but to our disappointment nobody showed up owing to not getting our telegraph[29]. We had to make the best of a bad job. We padded along asking for the Simpsons whom we found out at 12.30 to our disappointment had left there a long time ago. We now had to walk back again to town, a distance of about 3 miles and on getting some meat, we retired to bed in a hotel. We have since found our friends and made a start in a new world. I now draw to a close hoping the reader will find this useful if ever they intend leaving home.

I remain,
Yours S. Taylor

Sutherland did not, in the end, stay in the US for long before he

[28] The small Orkney island where Sutherland was born.
[29] Imagine the disappointment of travelling all that way, only to discover that the people to whom you were travelling had moved on!

retraced his tiring journey and returned home to Orkney. There, he married a girl from his native Flotta and established a successful general store in Kirkwall, the main Orcadian town. Sutherland died in Orkney in 1965.

You may have family papers describing the emigration experience of your own ancestors, but if not, the accounts of Stevenson and Sutherland each describe experiences of hardship and heartache that must surely have been universal. Departing from home, whether temporary or permanent, must have been a difficult, highly emotionally-charged thing to do but it was also associated in many cases with a sense of opportunity and excitement. The journey itself, in the 'temporary village' of an emigrant ship, will have been at best tedious and at worst terrifying, while the onward journey from the arrival port must have been frustratingly slow. This transition from one home to another was an important journey for your ancestors, making it a correspondingly important part of your own ancestral journey of discovery. The next chapter, Routes to Roots, will help you explore other parts of your ancestry.

CHAPTER 3

Routes to Roots: A Wealth of Information and Assistance

MORE AND MORE ANCESTRAL and genealogical research resources are becoming available to help you on your own journey of family discovery. In fact, there are so many sources now that finding the most useful ones can be bewildering and intimidating, particularly if you are only just beginning your research. You will find help and encouragement every step of the way, however, not least in the pages of this book. This chapter is intended to serve as an introduction to some of the ways in which you can get started in your search, and there are also tips for the more experienced researcher. Along the way we will look at resources – online and offline in the good old-fashioned real world – that can bring your Scottish ancestry and heritage to life for you.

There are many good introductions to ancestral research, some of which are listed in Appendix 1 at the end of this book. You may refer to them if you want detailed guidance on undertaking family research, especially genealogical research.

Bear in mind that this chapter is a personal selection derived from my own experience, from the questions asked most frequently at seminars and presentations, and from recommendations made by colleagues and fellow researchers. It is not an encyclopaedia of sources and makes no claims to be a definitive guide. You may have other favourites, discover new listings, or disagree with my selection. If so, please share this information with me via the *Rooted in Scotland* website: www. rootedinscotland.com.

The chapter is divided into two parts: in Part 1 you will find resources that are located in Scotland itself. Each one is described in an overview, followed by some comments – remember that this is personal opinion – and details of how to find out more, usually via a website. Where suggestions for further reading are made, full details of each book can be found in Appendix 1.

In Part 2 of the chapter we will review the resources available for ancestral researchers in other countries. There is inevitably less detail here, but enough to get you started on your ancestral journey.

If you are looking for general ancestral resources, rather than for specifically Scottish ones, there are two websites that, between them, will almost certainly be able to help. The first is www.ancestry.com, described as the most used genealogy site on the Web. With over 23,000 genealogical and historical databases, Ancestry.com is quite a phenomenon, part of a network of commercial sites including www.genealogy.com, www.familyhistory.com and www.ancestry. co.uk among others. The other useful starting point is Cyndi's List, www.cyndislist.com, an extremely comprehensive, free index to genealogical resources on the Web.

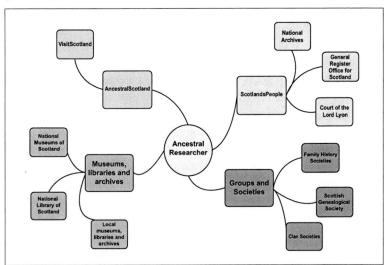

When considering the many ancestral research resources that are available, it can be useful to group the principal ones in order to assist with your research planning. This diagram shows the author's grouping of the main resources.

Part 1 – Routes to Roots in Scotland

I would like to introduce you to some of Scotland's many ancestral research resources, which are constantly being added to and developed further, making the past an exciting and dynamic place to explore.

Your Family

Your starting point in conducting family history research should always be you yourself. This is neither selfish nor egotistical; it is the most logical, common-sense way in which to start. Beginning with yourself, gather together information about your immediate relatives. Talk to as many of them as you can and write down what they say. If they have birth, marriage or death certificates, ask for copies. Write down family stories or – even better – make an audio or video recording. Family traditions and stories often have a basis in fact, even if some of the details get changed in the telling and re-telling of stories. Recording what you are told is an important step in preserving the past for the generations to come.

Family photographs are a wonderful resource. Get copies of them from your relatives and label the photographs so that dates, places and people are properly recorded, and do the same with any photographs you take from now on. Most families have small mountains of photographs but few of them are likely to be labelled in this way. How much more useful the photographs become when we know who is in them, where the photograph was taken, when, and on what occasion. Study these photographs carefully if you wish to use them as part of your ancestral research. Styles in photography have changed over time, particularly as the formal, portrait-style photography of Victorian times gave way to the more informal and candid style in use today. Detailed analysis of photographs takes time and effort, so write down what you learn from each photograph to leave a more accurate record of each.

If you are very lucky you may have access to letters, diaries or even autobiographies and biographies of family members. These can provide a fascinating insight into your ancestry, but you do need to approach these sources with care. With diaries, for example, did the writer expect other people to read the diary? If so, perhaps what they wrote was influenced by this knowledge. If I were to keep a diary and expected other people one day to read it, I would write about successes, not mistakes and uncertainties: do not take everything you read at face value. Reading between the lines for the fuller story and making judgements of this kind is something that historians are specially trained to do. It may not be easy, especially when you are dealing with your own ancestors.

Letters can be particularly useful in tracing your family's steps, though again, we need to keep in mind the reason or reasons behind why the letters were written. Very often you only have one half of the correspondence, which makes letters even harder to use as a source. Few of us keep copies of the letters we send, and email and text messaging nowadays have gone a long way towards reducing the number of letters written, so our descendants may have no opportunity to learn about us in the future from our correspondence.

We sometimes forget that before the telephone, email and text chat, letters were the main form of communication between people who could not talk directly to each other. One of my favourite letters in our local archive is dated 24 June 1874 and was sent from Canada to Orkney. It begins 'Your very kind letter of 23 June 1873 reached me on 31 March 1874....' – a whole year passed before the reply was sent! It is no surprise then that so many of our distant ancestors' letters begin with phrases such as 'We are all well though your cousin has been ill' and similar phrases. Whenever people received letters from their emigrated friends and relations, the first thing they would look for, surely, would be that sort of reassurance.

Comments

Birth, marriage and death certificates, census records, photos, diaries, letters and other tangible sources are the raw materials of ancestral research. Think of them as pieces of evidence in a detective mystery, or navigation points on the map of an ancestral journey. In assembling information from and about your family, make sure that the evidence you use is as accurate as possible. Historians make a distinction between primary sources, in other words, original records made at the time of an event, and secondary sources, which are other people's interpretation of events, generally made at a later time. You should always try to base your ancestral research on primary sources, checking and double checking everything, and backing it up by cross-referencing when available.

How to find out more

There are many helpful books about genealogy: I find Alwyn James' *Scottish Roots* and the late Kathleen Cory's *Tracing Your Scottish Ancestry* especially useful. For a broader perspective, the National Archives of Scotland's *Tracing Your Scottish Ancestors* provides an excellent guide to ancestry research in the National Archives.

If you are considering writing family history based on your ancestral research, I heartily recommend taking the Open University course 'A103 Start Writing Family History'. It runs several times a year, lasts twelve weeks and is available online so it can be done wherever and whenever you have a connection to the Internet. The course is more about history than genealogy but it is enjoyable and you will learn a great deal. Visit the Open University website www.open.ac.uk for more information.

The General Register Office for Scotland

www.gro-scotland.gov.uk

The General Register Office for Scotland is custodian of who we are. Without a doubt, it holds the most important Scottish family history records, and without its care and professionalism over so many years, and its commitment to supporting public access to ancestral research resources, Scotland would not now be the proud possessor of such high-quality and easily accessible records.

The General Register Office is a government agency with responsibility for the registration of births, marriages, civil partnerships, deaths, divorces and adoptions. It is also responsible for the ten-yearly census and for the publication of statistical information about Scotland's population and households. The system of civil registration in use today was introduced in 1855. Prior to this, baptisms or births, marriage banns or marriages and deaths or burials were recorded in what are known as the Old Parish Registers. The General Register Office for Scotland now has custody of these records, some of which date as far back as 1553, though these are exceptional. The survival of the Old Parish Registers varies between parts of Scotland and the quality of record-keeping – and indeed the amount of information recorded – was not the same as is the case with the modern civil registration system.

The earliest full Census of Scotland was that of 1841. Census records from then, up to and including 1901, are publicly available, but later censuses remain closed to the public until 100 years have elapsed. This provision is in place to protect the privacy of people whose information was recorded in the census and who may still be alive.

Ancestral researchers have three ways of accessing the resources of the General Register Office. First, they can visit a local Registrar in their geographical area of interest. These local Registrars, often found in local authority premises, have access to General Register Office databases and other information. Second, they can access the databases online via the website: www.scotlandspeople.gov.uk. Third, they can visit the main records repository at New Register House, located at the east end of Edinburgh's Princes Street. In an exciting development, the ScotlandsPeople website is being significantly enhanced at the same time as the New Register House and adjacent buildings are undergoing major (but sensitively done) building works to create what will be a state-of-the-art research centre.

Comments

The records maintained by the General Register Office for Scotland lie at the very heart of Scotland's rich ancestral research resources. A long-term programme of indexing and microfilming/digitisation has made many of the agency's records available online and protected the original records from damage or loss. There is something very special, though, about being in the actual building in which the original records are stored. You get an almost tangible sense of history in the search rooms and throughout the building.

How to find out more

At the General Register Office website, www.gro-scotland.gov.uk, you will find information about the services the agency provides and the family history resources in its custody. A very readable short history of the records in the General Register Office for Scotland is *Jock Tamson's Bairns* by Cecil Sinclair.

Scotlands People and the Scottish Family History Service Project

www.scotlandspeople.gov.uk

The www.scotlandspeople.gov.uk website is Scotland's pre-eminent ancestral research resource. The site is constantly being developed and new content added, but at the time of writing it has four main categories of records in its huge databases. First, there are the statutory registers of births, marriages and deaths dating from 1855 onwards. These are indexed and digital images of actual records are available. Second, there are records from the Old Parish Registers dating between 1553 – the earliest surviving register – and 1854. Third, there are census records from the 1841 to 1901 censuses. And fourth, thanks to collaboration between the General Register Office for Scotland and the National Archives of Scotland, indexed and digitised wills and testaments for the period 1513–1901 are also available.

The collaboration between these two partners has been extended to include the Court of the Lord Lyon, the heraldic court with responsibility for the *Public Register of all Arms and Bearings in Scotland*. These coats of arms are being digitised and indexed and will be available to search and view on the Scotlandspeople website in due course.

The collaboration goes further than that, however, and these three organisations are bringing their services together in a project known as the Scottish Family History Service, the aim of which is to create a one-stop focus for ancestral research, based at a new family history centre taking shape at General Register House and New Register House in Princes Street, Edinburgh. These magnificent buildings with their impressive Victorian domes are currently home to the project partners, operating separately, but refurbishment and redevelopment will physically integrate the buildings and make the integration of the project partners' services to visitors possible. This important development demonstrates the vast amount of interest there is in family history in Scotland and shows the determination of the General Register Office for Scotland, the National Archives of Scotland and the Court of the Lord Lyon to work together to keep Scotland at the forefront of ancestral research.

Comments

The www.scotlandspeople.gov.uk website provides access to the official records of Scotland's people, as well as a wealth of background information, help and advice. The availability of digital images of original records makes using the site a very satisfying and fully informative experience, wholly justifying the 'pay-per-view' basis on which it operates.

The Scottish Family History Service development is truly exciting, both in terms of the integration of the project partners' services and the creation of a world-class family history centre in Edinburgh. Ancestral researchers will be well served by the enhanced website and the new centre.

How to find out more

The Scotlandspeople website is regularly updated and there is a mailing list that you can join in order to keep up to date with news. For information on the Scottish Family History Service project, including a plan of the new centre and photographs of the building work, visit www.scotlandspeoplehub.gov.uk

Scottish Genealogy Society

www.scotsgenealogy.com

Founded in 1953, the Scottish Genealogy Society is based in Edinburgh in premises close to the historic Royal Mile. It promotes research into Scottish family history and has a splendid, comprehensive library and family history centre, use of which is free to members. Non-members pay a reasonable fee to use the facilities but for frequent users it makes more sense simply to join the Society and gain access to the benefits of membership, including a quarterly magazine *The Scottish Genealogist*. Membership fees are very reasonable.

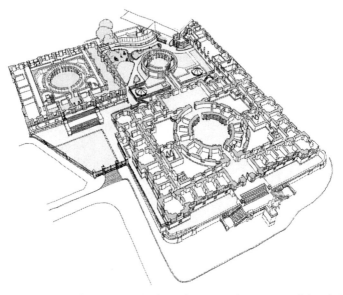

Perspective view of the new ScotlandsPeople Centre, Princes Street, Edinburgh. The Centre is due for completion in Autumn 2007.

Reproduced by kind permission of the ScotlandsPeople Centre.

The Society organises lectures and meetings, including group visits to the General Register Office. These visits are particularly useful because you are in the company of other enthusiasts and have the benefit of their support while you use the Register Office facilities.

The Society has a good website, located at www.scotsgenealogy.com which includes three elements of particular use for people who cannot visit the premises in Edinburgh in person. First, there is an online shop with some 1,400 publications available; members receive a discount on purchases. Second, there is an information section with a rather eclectic selection of useful articles, well worth browsing through. You will be surprised how much of it may be useful in your own research. Finally, there is also an online forum. This is a relatively new development on the website and is an excellent place to post queries or, indeed, to post answers to other people's questions.

Comments

The Scottish Genealogy Society is a very reputable, committed and knowledgeable body with a library and family history centre which is, in its quiet way, an inspirational place to visit. I value my own membership of the Society and would encourage other ancestral researchers to join.

How to find out more

The Society welcomes personal visitors at its library and family history centre in Edinburgh. Opening times and further information about the Society and its activities can be found at www. scotsgenealogy.com.

Family History Societies

www.safhs.org.uk

Family History Societies are at the heart of ancestral research at a local level in Scotland. There are societies covering every part of Scotland and, though the societies vary in size and the extent of their activities, they each maintain a variety of research resources including family trees, newsletters, monumental inscriptions and occasional research publications. Most hold regular meetings at which visitors are always very welcome, and many societies are able to provide research assistance to members.

It is perhaps this research assistance that is potentially of most use to you as an ancestral researcher. Society members who live in the area will have an intimate knowledge of place names, notable families, other researchers and so on: a real wealth of local knowledge. I have benefited personally from my own local society's depth of knowledge – a casual mention of the name of my grandfather's boat triggered a memory on the part of a fellow member. 'Let me think about this, I'm sure I have something' he said, and within three days he had searched through his own files and found information about the boat, including when it was built, where it sailed and when it was sold. That sort of local knowledge is invaluable.

Comments

Family history societies typically have members who live in the local area, as well as other members who live elsewhere but whose ancestors came from the area. This mix of people helps make society newsletters very cosmopolitan and lively rather than inward-looking, and the information that can potentially be gained by this networking is invaluable. Membership of family history societies is not expensive, so joining is highly recommended.

How to find out more

Most societies have a website and there are links to these from the website of the Scottish Association of Family History Societies www.safhs.org.uk. Alternatively, there are links from the ancestral tourism website www.ancestralscotland.com and the 'Genuki' site www.genuki.org.uk, which is described in more detail below.

Genuki

www.genuki.org.uk

Genuki – **Gen**ealogy **U**nited **Ki**ngdom and Ireland – is an astonishing phenomenon. Launched in 1995, it is the oldest and largest genealogical site devoted to the British Isles, with around 55,000 pages of information maintained by an army of volunteers. Genuki aims to provide a comprehensive collection of ancestral research information. Its coverage is much wider than genealogy in the strict sense, so it is a tremendously useful resource for ancestral researchers, whatever the focus of their interest. While there is some general information, the real strength of Genuki, and the depth of information content, is in the local information.

For each part of the UK and Ireland, Genuki is organised by county and, within each county, by parish. Note, though, that parish-level information is by no means complete, but this is not a great problem for the determined researcher.

Comments

Genuki is very useful, but because it is maintained by volunteers, the quality and depth of material can vary from county to county. This is not a problem so long as you are prepared to use Genuki as a starting point and not as a definitive, authoritative guide without any further investigation.

To get the best from Genuki, start by looking at the advice for first time users and the guidance on how information is presented. Bear in mind that the site is designed to provide information so it doesn't have the slick design values and rich graphics that you'll find on many other sites, though personally I think that this is one of the virtues of Genuki – it achieves what its founding trustees set out to do.

How to find out more

The Genuki website is www.genuki.org.uk. Just follow the links once you are there, and you'll find a mass of helpful information, though take care not to get lost down some of the fascinating highways and byways you'll discover along your ancestral journey.

The International Genealogical Index

www.familysearch.org

The International Genealogical Index (IGI) is one of the world's largest collections of genealogical records, created from a number of different sources including the results of individual research and original records.

The IGI was created and is maintained by members of the

Church of Jesus Christ of Latter-day Saints, more commonly known as the Mormons. Family is of fundamental importance to the Mormons and members of the church are actively involved in family history research. The Family History Library in Salt Lake City, Utah, is the main repository for the information collected by Mormon researchers. There are also some 4,000 branches of the library, known as Family History Centres, throughout the world. At the time of writing there are 15 Mormon Family History Centres in Scotland alone, from Lerwick in the north to Dumfries in the south.

Comments

The Mormons' family history website at www.familysearch.org is free to use and can be a useful way of making progress with your ancestral research. Bear in mind, though, that the IGI is not complete and because of human error it contains factual mistakes as well as transcription errors. You should always double check IGI information using original records, preferably official ones. If you do find errors in the IGI do let one of the Family History Centres know so that the records can be corrected for the benefit of other researchers.

How to find out more

The Church of Jesus Christ of Latter-day Saints provides online access to information via its website www.familysearch.org The importance attached to ancestral research is clear from the placement of a search facility on the home page of the site.

Maps

Maps are an especially useful ancestral research resource. Knowing the name of a place where an ancestor lived is one thing, but being able to find the location on a map, especially an old map, can help give you a real feeling of connection with the place. That sense of connection – the feeling of being rooted in a particular part of Scotland, is what this book is all about.

The National Library of Scotland has a large and wonderful collection of historic maps, about 4,000 of which are available on the Library's website at www.nls.uk/digitallibrary/map as digital images. Maps from as early as 1560 can be viewed, enabling you to see how Scotland's regions, towns and latterly cities have developed over time.

The Ordnance Survey is Britain's national mapping agency. As well as modern maps, it also has a large archive of historic maps and many of these are now available online via www.old-maps.co.uk These 19th century maps may well help with your ancestral research, not least when you come to write a family history and need to be able to show where your ancestors lived.

Comments

By using maps, whether historic ones or more modern ones, you will be able to associate the *people* whose births, marriages and deaths form the backbone of your family tree with the *places* in which they lived and loved and reached the end of their lives. Maps are, then, an essential part of your ancestral research.

Remember that place names sometimes changed over time. Places, houses, even whole streets might disappear from later maps. If your ancestor was a crofter in the Highlands, for example, and was a victim of the controversial Clearances, the ruins of their croft or village might not survive today, but they may still be visible on 19th century maps.

How to find out more

The National Library of Scotland's digital map collection can be accessed at www.nls.uk/digitallibrary/maps and the Ordnance

Survey First edition maps at www.old-maps.co.uk. Genuki, www. genuki.org.uk, may have information about other maps covering your area of interest, and don't forget to ask at the relevant local archive or library, or the local family history society. For modern maps of Scotland many ancestral researchers will already be familiar with www.streetmap.co.uk or www.multimap.com. Finally, have a look at www.mapyourancestors.com. We are likely to see further developments in this sort of mapping in the future.

The Royal Commission

www.rcahms.gov.uk

To give it its full name, the Royal Commission on the Ancient and Historical Monuments of Scotland is responsible for 'recording, interpreting and collecting information about the built environment in Scotland'. Despite its rather intimidating name – often abbreviated to RCAHMS – this is an under-utilised but potentially rewarding ancestral research resource.

The Commission takes an interest in archaeology, architecture and history and it has a large collection of material, much of it accessible at the RCAHMS library in Edinburgh. There, a team of enthusiastic, knowledgeable staff will do their best to help you find what you are looking for. While you are unlikely to find material that relates directly to your family tree, there is much amongst the several million items in the collections that might have an indirect connection. For instance, there is an impressive collection of historical aerial photography and your ancestors' houses or streets might be visible.

As well as providing services at its premises in Edinburgh, RCAHMS produces a range of publications and has a website that it is worth exploring thoroughly. There are four databases which are of interest to ancestral researchers. CANMORE contains details of about a quarter of a million archaeological sites, monuments and maritime sites in Scotland, together with an index of drawings, manuscripts and photographs. PASTMAP contains national and regional archaeological and architectural data. AIR-PHOTOFINDER will help you locate relevant aerial photography and HLAMAP contains historic land use assessment information. Depending on the direction and depth of your ancestral research one or more of these databases may be of interest.

Comments

The RCAHMS library is something of a hidden treasure, well worth a visit if you are in Edinburgh and want to broaden your under-standing of Scotland's built heritage, and the website can be very useful if you are doing your research at a distance.

How to find out more

The website of the Royal Commission on the Ancient and Historical Monuments of Scotland can be found at www.rcahms.gov.uk. If you wish to explore Scotland's built environment further you should also look at www.historic-scotland.gov.uk: Historic Scotland's work is closely related to that of RCAHMS.

National Archives of Scotland

www.nas.gov.uk

The mission of the National Archives of Scotland (NAS) includes to 'select, preserve and make available the national archives of Scotland': this is indeed an important mission. We encountered the National Archives earlier in the context of the development of the Scottish Family History Service, a joint initiative with the General Register Office for Scotland and the Court of the Lord Lyon, though there is space for only a brief introduction to NAS here. The main National Archives of Scotland website is www.nas.gov.uk and this provides a great deal of information about the archives' holdings. There is access to an online catalogue on the website, though you must bear in mind that it has not yet proved possible to convert all the paper-based catalogues into digital form. Nevertheless the catalogue will let you identify many items of interest prior to a visit to the archive itself.

In addition to catalogues of its own material, NAS is also responsible for the National Register of Archives for Scotland, a record of significant papers in private hands. You can search a catalogue of this material online via the NAS website.

Thanks to a major project known as the Scottish Archive Network (SCAN) you are able, in addition, to search an electronic catalogue of the material held in over 50 public archives in Scotland. There is a dedicated website, www.scan.org.uk, where you can do this. It is well worth exploring this as its knowledge base alone is an invaluable source of information and inspiration, never mind the wealth of advice and expertise that is available throughout this excellent site. The SCAN project was responsible for the large-scale digitisation of records comprising Scottish Wills and Testaments now forming part of the ScotlandsPeople website described earlier.

SCAN also maintains another fascinating and useful site on behalf of the National Archives of Scotland, www.scottishhandwriting.com. This site is designed to help you get to grips with reading manuscript historical documents dating from 1500 to 1750. The site provides tutorials and coaching, and this is a fun way to improve your understanding of historical documents as well as providing useful information.

Comments

As you would expect, given that Scotland has such excellent archival records, the National Archives of Scotland provides a first-class service via its websites and also in person when researchers use either of the NAS buildings in central Edinburgh. Note that in order to use the NAS' facilities you will need to get a reader's ticket. These are only available when you visit in person: remember to bring proof of your identity and address.

How to find out more

The NAS website, www.nas.gov.uk is probably the best starting point for finding out more, as there are links from there to all the other websites mentioned above. The official guide to local history research in the National Archives is Cecil Sinclair's *Tracing Scottish Local History.*

National Library of Scotland

www.nls.uk

The imposing, almost forbidding exterior of the National Library of Scotland building on George IV Bridge in Edinburgh belies the richness of the collection the library holds and the helpfulness of the professional staff. The National Library (NLS) has been described as one of the great libraries of the world and is the world's leading centre for the study of Scotland and its people. There are millions of books, manuscripts, music and maps occupying over 110 miles of shelving – a real treasure-house for researchers.

Online catalogues accessible via the Library's website make searching easy and enable you to identify material of interest well in advance of a visit to the library. If your research interest is the Scottish diaspora then you will find the 'Scots Abroad' section of the online catalogues especially helpful. Here you will find databases relating to topics such as the Scots in North America, Emigrants' Guides and Emigrants' Correspondence. While it is unlikely that you will find direct references to your own ancestors in these documents – although that is always possible – the real value of the collection lies in the intimate, contemporary detail bringing to life the actual experience of emigration.

Emigrants' Guides were written for a particular purpose, so these are not unbiased sources, but the emigrants' correspondence – most of it dating from the 19th and 20th centuries – can be very absorbing and touching. In their letters people share their hopes, fears and uncertainties and, through their words, we can reach some understanding of the actual experience of emigration.

The NLS map collection, one of the largest in the world, was introduced earlier in this chapter. If you are planning to use the map library in person, do remember that it is housed in a separate building on Causewayside in Edinburgh, rather than in the George IV Bridge building which houses the main NLS reading rooms.

Comments

The National Library of Scotland is a wonderful resource for anyone interested in any aspect of Scotland, but it is particularly useful for ancestral researchers wishing to broaden their research out from the story of their own family and relate that story to the wider sweep of Scottish history at home and abroad.

In order to use the reading rooms at the main NLS building on George IV Bridge you will need a reader's ticket but you can download and complete the application in advance to save time when you arrive. Once you have a reader's ticket, you can pre-order some post-1800 books online, enabling you to make the best use of your time when you visit.

How to find out more

The NLS website (www.nls.uk) is an excellent way to learn more about the National Library and begin to access its incredibly rich collection. If your childhood memories are of libraries being stuffy, dry and boring, then prepare to have that perception changed.

The Mitchell Library

www.mitchelllibrary.org

Glasgow's Mitchell Library has grown from its beginnings, with a collection of 14,000 books in 1877, to its current status as one of Europe's largest public reference libraries with over 1.3 million books. The Mitchell, as it is known, is an institution at the very heart of Glasgow's history and the collection housed in the library is a first-class resource for researchers.

Among the records in the Archives and Special Collections of the Mitchell are burial records, poor law archives and church and school archives, as well as census records and a wealth of other material including the extensive city archives. One way to get to grips with the overwhelming amount of material held by The Mitchell is to attend one of the regular family history surgeries. At the time of writing these are held on the first Thursday of every month, starting at 5.30 p.m. The surgeries are free and there is no need to book a place in advance.

If you are unable to visit The Mitchell in person you may find the resources of the appropriately named Virtual Mitchell of use. Here, at www.mitchelllibrary.org, you can search by area, street, subject or just browse through the large collection of fascinating photographs.

Comments

The Mitchell has a truly impressive range of resources and services. In an ambitious project, the Mitchell Library and Theatre complex is being extensively redeveloped, retaining the character of the magnificent buildings but making them fit for the expectations and demands of the 21st century. The work is being done in phases so check before you visit The Mitchell.

How to find out more

Information about the Mitchell Library can be found on the Glasgow City Council website at www.glasgow.gov.uk/en/visitors/familyhistory/. The site also contains details of other useful resources, particularly the Strathclyde Genealogy Centre. The Virtual Mitchell site, enabling online searching, is www.mitchell library.org. If you are interested in the history of Glasgow itself – essential if your ancestors lived in the city – then The Glasgow Story (www.theglasgowstory.com) provides a lively introduction. Use the Quick Search facility if you are looking for specific information.

The Statistical Accounts of Scotland

http://edina.ac.uk

There have been three so-called 'statistical accounts' of Scotland, but only the first two are of special interest to ancestral researchers. The first account, sometimes referred to as the Old Statistical Account (OSA), was based on parish-by-parish reports prepared by local ministers and was published between 1791 and 1799. The second account, referred to as the New Statistical Account (NSA) and once again based on local information, was published between 1834 and 1845. Most recently, the *Third Statistical Account of Scotland* was published between 1951 and 1992.

Remember Sutherland Simpson Taylor, whom we met in Chapter 2, as he undertook his long journey from Flotta in Orkney to Seattle? The Old and New Statistical Accounts can give us valuable information about his native Flotta in the years before Sutherland's birth. In the OSA the Reverend James Bremner of Flotta parish tells us that: 'The people are very peaceable and inoffensive, apparently very simple but in fact abundantly shrewd.'[30] Later, in the NSA, the Reverend Walter Weir says of Flotta: 'This island is particularly well suited for fishing; and the inhabitants, who are very enterprising, have excellent boats, and yield to no seaman in managing them. They are industrious, and when not detained at home by their farming operations, they are engaged in fishing, which to them is a more pleasing and profitable employment.'[31]

---

[30] Page 320, volume 17, Account of 1791-99:
http://stat-acc-scot.edina.ac.uk/link/1791-99/Orkney/Walls%20and%20Flotta/17/320/
[31] Page 77, volume 15, Account of 1834–45:
http://stat-acc-scot.edina.ac.uk/link/1834-45/Orkney/Walls%20and%20Flotta/15/77/

While it is unlikely that the OSA or the NSA will provide details directly about your ancestors, information – like the above excerpts that detail the character of the community into which Sutherland was born – of this sort is both intriguing and enlightening when considering the lifestyles of your forebears.

Comments

Reading these snapshot accounts of the places your ancestors lived is a good way to help understand their lives and times. Of course the accounts are unlikely to mention your ancestors by name but even so, knowing what the area was like based on a first-hand description can give you a real feeling of connection.

How to find out more

The Statistical Accounts run to several volumes each – the Old Account, for example, consists of twenty-one volumes – and they are available in many libraries and study centres. But the easiest way to get access to the documents is via the Edina website at http://edina.ac.uk, where digitised pages of both the Old and New Statistical Accounts can be browsed free of charge. Edina is an academic service based at Edinburgh University and, while many of the resources on the website are intended for academic use only, you do not need to register to use the Accounts. They are an enormously useful and popular resource.

Newspapers

http://archive.scotsman.com

Most of us who read newspapers do so in order to keep up with what is happening, whether on the international, national or local level. We may browse through the intimations of births, marriages and deaths, or home straight in on favourite sections of the paper.

Reading through old newspapers is a very good way to deepen your understanding of the world your ancestors knew, and local archives and study centres are likely to have such newspapers in their collections. Some family history societies or individual researchers may even have indexed individual newspapers, making them much easier to use as a source of ancestry-related information.

Perhaps the most impressive, and certainly the most useful, newspaper-based project is *The Scotsman*'s digital archive. *The Scotsman* newspaper, which first appeared in 1817 in Edinburgh, has become a national institution. Following a massive programme of digitisation and indexing, the entire newspaper archive from 1817 to 1950 is now available online at http:// archive.scotsman.com. If any of your ancestors were listed in a news story or in a birth, marriage or death notice, you will be able to use the free search facility to find them. To view full articles, however, you will need to purchase a subscription. As well as the search facility on the website, there are helpful tips, timelines and special articles of interest to ancestral researchers.

Comments

Newspapers are a great way to bring a period in history to life, and if you are able to find an ancestor mentioned in the newspaper this is a real bonus. *The Scotsman*'s digital archive is an especially useful resource; although it is Edinburgh-based, it carries news from throughout Scotland.

How to find out more

To find out which local newspapers covered your geographical area of interest, have a look at the relevant county pages on the Genuki website, where you'll find a list of relevant publications. Alternatively, ask the appropriate local family history society for advice.

National Museums of Scotland

www.nms.ac.uk

As the name suggests, the National Museums of Scotland comprises several museums, not just one. The Royal Museum and the Museum of Scotland stand side by side in Edinburgh's Chambers Street. The Royal Museum houses international collections of decorative arts, science and industry, archaeology and the natural world. It occupies a truly impressive Victorian building and is one of the most pleasant places in Edinburgh to sit and relax.

The Museum of Scotland, a striking contemporary building, is a must for anyone wanting to understand the story of Scotland's land, people and culture. The Museum is divided into a number of galleries, each with a character of its own – you will want to spend some time exploring the Industry and Empire gallery but all of the galleries are fascinating.

If the focus of your interest is Scotland's rural heritage, then the Museum of Scottish Country Life at Kittochside (between East Kilbride and Glasgow) gives you the opportunity to visit a working farm and museum. Alternatively, if Scotland's more modern history holds your interest, the Museum of Flight at East Fortune Airfield in East Lothian is also worth a visit.

Finally, fashion and social etiquette from the 1850s to the 1950s is presented at the Shambellie House Museum of Costume in Dumfriesshire. It is fascinating to see how fashions in clothing have changed: a visit here can be especially interesting if you have old photographs of ancestors wearing period costume. With such artefacts, you can use your visit to find out more about their social and economic station through their style of dress. You will be surprised how much more you can understand about the past by doing so.

Comments

The Royal Museum and Museum of Scotland are both free, but

there are very reasonable entry fees at the Museum of Scottish Country Life and Shambellie House. Visits to each of the museums are recommended. As well as the museums' permanent exhibits keep an eye out for special exhibitions, events and lectures. These are often of interest to ancestral researchers and sometimes touch directly on Scottish emigration. Other museums dotted around Scotland – for example, the Mining Museum outside Edinburgh, the New Lanark mill outside Glasgow, and the Verdant Works museum related to weaving in Dundee – are also excellent sources of information if you know that your ancestors were involved in a particular industry, and we will touch on this below

How to find out more

The best way to find out more is at the National Museums of Scotland website, www.nms.ac.uk.

Scottish Museums Council

www.scottishmuseums.org.uk

It may seem strange to include the Scottish Museums Council (SMC) here; after all, it doesn't actually run any museums itself, but in fact it plays an absolutely vital role in Scotland's museums and galleries. It is the membership body for Scotland's non-national museums and galleries, providing them with a range of services, support and encouragement.

More people visit museums and galleries than any other type of visitor attraction in Scotland. Local museums can provide an intimate introduction to their native area and many of them benefit from elderly volunteers who have a deep knowledge of earlier generations and of life in the area 'the way it was'. The SMC website, www.scottishmuseums.org.uk, has a very useful search facility that enables you to select an area of Scotland and view details of the SMC member museums in that area.

Recognising the growing interest in ancestral research and the important part that museums have to play in helping researchers find out more about their Scottish ancestry, SMC worked with a group of Scottish industrial museums and others on a project to address the increasing amount of ancestry-related enquiries with which museums are now dealing. One of the outcomes of the project was a series of fact sheets providing advice for people whose ancestors worked as coal miners, fishermen, jute workers, lead miners, at New Lanark cotton mill, in maritime industries or on the railways. If you know or suspect that your ancestor(s) worked in one of those industries, view the news article dated 8 June 2006 at www.scottishmuseums.co.uk.

Comments

Museum collections can help you understand your ancestors' lives, and Scotland is lucky both in the number of good museums located here and in the proactive professional support that these receive from the Scottish Museums Council.

How to find out more

Visiting the SMC website, www.scottishmuseums.org.uk, provides an introduction to the work of the Museums Council, as well as enabling you to search for member museums by name or by area.

Heritage Visitor Attractions

Every visitor attraction potentially has some appeal for ancestral researchers depending on their particular focus of interest. With the amount of available information on this subject, this chapter is not intended for use as a methodical guide to Scotland's visitor attractions, but it will introduce you to three attractions that I believe are particularly useful to the ancestral researcher. The first of these is the Highland Folk Museum, located on two sites – Kingussie and Newtonmore – in the Cairngorms National Park. This award-winning museum provides a fascinating insight into Highland life as it was in the past. The core of the Folk Museum's collection is in Kingussie where, in addition to displays of artefacts, you can look around a traditional blackhouse and speak to one of the costumed guides. The other part of the museum, a living history museum incorporating a working farm, is located in Newtonmore. The reconstructed 1700s township is an evocative, thought-provoking part of the living history complex. It feels like another world – the world in which our ancestors lived.

The second useful site is the Strathnaver Museum on the north coast of the county of Sutherland. Here we are in Mackay Country, the Province of Strathnaver, where the once-powerful Clan Mackay had its heartlands. On one occasion I met an elderly gentleman here, who introduced himself as: 'I'm a Mackay; in the land of Mackay.' For this Mr Mackay, the memory of the Highland Clearances was still raw, just a few generations after the actual events that saw Strathnaver cleared of its people, pushed to coastal fringes such as Bettyhill. In addition to the fascinating artefacts and archive, housed in an attractive former church dating from 1700, the Strathnaver Museum is an ideal place from which to embark on the 26-mile long Strathnaver Trail, a driving trail and accompanying leaflet that will introduce you to the remains of 6,000 years of human occupation of the Strathnaver valley.

Finally, there is perhaps the most evocative of sites, Culloden Moor, where in 1746 the dreams of young Bonnie Prince Charlie were shattered and the brutal repression of the Highlands began. Located near the city of Inverness, the National Trust for Scotland manages the site and a major new visitor centre and re-interpretation of the battlefield will open in summer 2007. The very latest research will inform this new interpretation, which will raise challenging questions about identity, social values, and about the migration of so many of Scotland's people from their troubled homeland in the 18th century. If you want to understand

Scotland, particularly its Highland past, then a visit to Culloden is an absolute necessity whether your ancestors fought for the Government or the rebels.

Comments

Heritage visitor attractions can bring the past to life in ways that written documents, no matter how personal in nature, cannot. Well worth a visit, you will get so much more from your forays to heritage attractions if you do some research in advance and come with some questions in mind.

How to find out more

You can find out more about the Highland Folk Museum at http://highlandfolk.museum. For the Strathnaver Museum look at www.strathnavermuseum.org.uk, and for more on Mackay Country, especially if you have Mackay ancestors, go to www.mackaycountry.com. The National Trust for Scotland site www.nts.org.uk has information about the current Culloden visitor centre, or for information about the Culloden Battlefield Memorial Project visit www.culloden.org. Finally, for information about Scotland's many (and varied) visitor attractions with most relevance for ancestral researchers, go to www.ancestralscotland.com where you will find attractions listed for each county.

Clans

In Scottish Gaelic, the word *clann* means 'children', and has come to mean 'family' as a tribal, Celtic concept. In the Celtic world, land belonged to a tribe and the tribal leader held power as a sort of trust – his role was to protect the land and people of the tribe, and to lead them. In Gaelic, the collective heritage of the clan was known as the *duthchas*, the right to settle territories over which the chiefs provided protection. Unlike feudal society, in which authority was handed down from the monarch, in a traditional clan system the authority of the Chief came from *within* the clan itself – a system that was regarded by the monarchy as a threat to the feudal order. The compromise reached in Scotland was the convention that the king was called 'High King', or Chief of Chiefs, but in reality internal clan loyalty was given first and foremost to the clan chief, not to the king.

Clans are usually regarded as a Highland phenomenon and associated with the Gaelic language, but the idea of clan as family was known in the Lowlands as well. The clan structure was hierarchical, with the Chief and lairds, the so-called 'big men', supported by 'tacksmen'. The latter were lesser gentry or 'middle managers', to give them a more modern comparison. Below them were the bulk of the population of the clan's lands and, inevitably, the lower you were down the pecking order, the harder your life was likely to be.

The tacksmen are a fascinating group. While the modern successful corporation depends upon the quality of its middle managers, so too were the success of clans based upon the efficacy of their tacksmen. There are suggestions that successful mass emigrations of Scots to North America were at least facilitated by tacksmen, if not directly organised by them. There might be a fruitful question for further research there – the role of tacksmen as middle managers and their impact on the us's development as a global economic power is a subject ripe for future discussion.

The legal position of the clan is interesting and worth noting. A clan is a legally recognised entity if it has an officially recognised chief or head who is a nobleman of Scotland. In other words, it has a corporate identity in law, and is the chief's heritable property. The arms of the clan (which we shall discuss in more detail below) are the personal property of the chief, and it is against the law for anyone other than the chief to use them. A name group, in contrast, which has no chief, has no legal identity. The Clan Muir, for example, has not had a Chief for 300 years. Thanks to the efforts of the Clan Muir Society, however, it now has a 'Head of the House of Muir' and hopes in time to apply to the Lord Lyon for 'rematriculation' of arms, enabling it to have a legitimate Chief once more.

Comments

The idea of clans has a renewed importance today. As clan and family societies find new energy and purpose, they help create a global network of people with a shared heritage. Clan societies and Highland Games do a great deal of good, transcending national boundaries and bringing people together from across the globe. To put it simply, clans still matter.

The clans are associated with the wearing of tartan, the colourful cloth that has become a Scottish icon. We will leave a discussion of tartan until a later chapter, in which we will examine it alongside other aspects of Scottish culture and identity. For now, though, we will just note that unique patterns of tartan are associated with each clan, enabling clan members to show their affiliation to the body visually via the tartan they choose to wear.

How to find out more

A good, colourfully-illustrated introduction to clans is *Scottish Clan and Family Names* by Roddy Martine. An introduction to the clan system and a search facility enabling you to find out more about your own clan can be found at www.myclan.com, the official website of the Standing Council of Scottish Chiefs, while the Ancestral Scotland website, www.ancestralscotland.com, also provides clan information and a clan search facility. Special clan-themed touring itineraries are available for download from this site.

Heraldry

www.lyon-court.com

Heraldry, also called armory, has its origins in 12th century

Europe. In an age of widespread illiteracy, the use of unique visual emblems to represent individuals was a way for the great and the good to identify themselves and to differentiate one another from their competitors in a clear and easily understood way. Sound familiar? In the modern world, we can relate this to the marketing concept of branding. It is sometimes said that marketing is like warfare – in heraldry, warfare is like marketing: it is all about image.

In Scottish heraldry, the most significant person is the Lord Lyon King of Arms, who exercises, on behalf of the Sovereign (from whom all honour is said to flow) a heraldic, genealogical and ceremonial role. Applications for grants of arms – i.e. requests for coats of arms – are made by petition to the Lord Lyon, who acts as a court of law and whose decision in heraldic matters is final. The Lord Lyon maintains the *Public Register of all Arms and Bearings in Scotland*, in which a magnificent painted version of each coat of arms is recorded and displayed, but which also includes a detailed written description of each coat of arms. These descriptions are made using a strict, specialised and highly structured terminology called blazon. The stricture of terminology used in each description is necessary due to heraldry's place as a matter of law in Scotland, (a great difference to England, where heraldry is not legality.)

An important point to note is that grants of arms in Scotland are personal: there is no such thing as a family coat of arms, or indeed a clan coat of arms. While clans are recognised by the Sovereign and distinguished by heraldry, the clan Chief's coat of arms belongs exclusively to him or her, and thus may only be used by them. The Chief of the clan may bear the clan arms, but must first prove his or her right to them to the satisfaction of the Lord Lyon. Because it is illegal to use arms that don't belong to you, there is only one way in which clan members can use a heraldic device: the clan badge, also known as the 'strap and buckle' or the 'clansman's crest badge'. In form, it is the Chief's crest surrounded by a fastened belt and buckle on which the clan motto is displayed. (Again, there are strict rules regarding its use. It cannot, for example, be used on a clansman's stationery.) The clan badge can be worn daily and particularly on ceremonial occasions by clan members to publicly show their allegiance to the Chief.

Comments

Heraldry is a fascinating area. Each coat of arms is a work of art, rich in symbolism and beautiful to look at. Some would say that heraldry is an anachronism in today's world, a throwback to medieval times, but it is in reality a living tradition and an important part of the fabric of Scotland and its history.

How to find out more

The Court of the Lord Lyon is working with other partners as part of the Family History Service described earlier in this chapter. As part of this project, coats of arms have been digitised and indexed and will be searchable as part of the www.scotlandspeople.gov.uk resource. The Court's own website is www.lyon-court.com, providing a colourful introduction to the work of the Lord Lyon and his colleagues. A good short guide to heraldry in Scotland is *Scotland's Heraldic Heritage* by Charles Burnett and Mark Dennis.

Electric Scotland

www.electricscotland.com

Electric Scotland is a Scottish interest website, created and managed by Alastair McIntyre, which is included here because it contains a huge amount of information – more than 20,000 pages' worth – covering a variety of Scottish and Scots-Irish topics. It is not an 'official' website, though McIntyre has arranged to leave the site to the Scottish Studies Foundation in Guelph, Ontario (near Toronto) when he retires, which will ensure that the site content is maintained for its hundreds of thousands of visitors.

There is so much information on Electric Scotland that it can be difficult to know where to start, so a good place to begin is by exploring your own interests. Bear in mind, as usual, that you should double check any information that you plan to incorporate into your own family tree, preferably by going to the original official source.

Comments

Alastair McIntyre has created a fascinating, quirky website overflowing with information at Electric Scotland. You will want to make your own judgement about whether the site suits your interests and the way in which you like to learn about Scotland and its people, but I find it useful as a general introduction to topics, following up any areas of interest it generates in more detail using other resources.

How to find out more

The Electric Scotland website is at www.electricscotland.com, and more information about its founder, Alastair McIntyre, may be found at www.electricscotland.net.

Professional Genealogists

www.asgra.co.uk

Professional researchers can be very effective, especially if you are not confident in your own research skills, don't have time to do the research, or need access to records that are not available online. The Association of Scottish Genealogists and Researchers in Archives (ASGRA) represents qualified and experienced searchers working personally in Scotland. They agree to adhere to a strict Code of Practice, assuring the quality of their work. Note, though, that ASGRA members are individuals, which means that operators of ancestral research businesses are not represented by the Association. This is a pity, and is potentially confusing for people who use research services. There are several ancestral research businesses in Scotland. The General Register Office for Scotland can provide a list on request, or you can find their details by performing an Internet search on Google. You will have to make your own judgement as to the suitability of your chosen researcher prior to commissioning any work from him or her, and it is always a good idea to ask for feedback from previous clients before doing so.

Comments

Professional researchers, by definition, charge for their services and the onus is therefore on you to check their credentials carefully before commissioning. The first step is to be very clear regarding the service you wish to purchase and the information that you expect them to find, then try and get personal recommendations from previous users on which to base your decision. Prepare as much information for the researcher as you can, as that will save them time so long as you can assure them that what you have done has been thorough and is carefully checked.

How to find out more

For more about ASGRA look at the Association's website at www. asgra.co.uk, or visit the General Register Office for Scotland online at www.gro-scotland.gov.uk.

Some researchers advertise in popular magazines such as *Family History Monthly*, *Family Tree Magazine* and *History Scotland*. To get an idea of the range of services and fees charged by a well-known research business, Scottish Roots, visit www.scottish-roots.com.

AncestralScotland

www.ancestralscotland.com

While we will visit the ancestral tourism phenomenon later on, it is worth noting here that Scotland's national tourism agency, VisitScotland, recognised the tourism potential of the increasing worldwide interest in ancestral connections some years ago and developed the AncestralScotland website as a result. Unlike traditional tourism websites, AncestralScotland provides access to research resources – some of them on the site itself – in order to help you take your genealogical research further. Not unnaturally, those behind the AncestralScotland initiative hope that you will want to come home to Scotland to see it for yourself, and in that they are quite correct. It may be a cliché to say so, but the journey of discovery that is ancestral research will quite naturally – almost inevitably – lead you back to the places your ancestors lived.

AncestralScotland seeks to enable you to make that ancestral journey. The site provides a mix of encouragement, guidance and some really useful simple searches. The surname search may show you where your surname was most common in Scotland at the end of the 19th century. This can help focus your research if you are at the very start of your research journey. And the place name search can help pin down specific locations that might be mentioned in family papers in your possession.

Many people of Scottish ancestry are interested in finding out more about their ancestral clan, and the AncestralScotland website helps you do this via a clan search facility. This will show you where your clan heartland was, give you a short history of the clan and its tartan and provide links to further information. Elsewhere on the site you will find a number of clan itineraries: downloadable touring itineraries that guide you to the main places in Scotland associated with your clan, enabling you to base all or part of a visit to Scotland around these suggested sites.

Comments

The philosophy behind the AncestralScotland initiative is a fairly sensitive one, very different to the 'exploiting a market' thinking that underlies many other parts of tourism promotional activity. At

AncestralScotland, the idea is that by helping people get started with their research and by enabling them to get the very best from the heritage journey to Scotland that they eventually make, ancestral tourists will be encouraged to return more frequently, stay longer when they do and will ultimately, spend more money while in Scotland.

How to find out more

The AncestralScotland website is regularly refined and updated to make sure that it keeps abreast of changing needs and expectations, and that it reflects developments in other online ancestral research resources.

Part 2 – Routes to Roots in Other Countries

You will find people of Scottish ancestry almost everywhere in the world, even if sometimes the passing of generations has led to some connections being forgotten. In these instances, the ancestral journey may be a revelation to family researchers, rather than a confirmation of what they suspected or knew.

The Scottish connection is probably at its deepest in the US, Canada, New Zealand, and Australia, or at least the memory of the connection is at its strongest, though it does echo strongly in England and Ireland too. This part of the chapter provides short introductions to getting started with ancestral research in each of these countries. If you are beginning your search in these areas, I hope your footsteps lead you back to Scotland.

United States of America

The US has been described as a nation of emigrants. Certainly there is a long tradition of emigration from Scotland across the Atlantic – you met Sutherland Taylor in the last chapter, for instance, whose experience was typical of thousands of others. For background reading on this subject, Jenni Calder's highly readable book, *Scots in the USA* provides an up-to-date historical perspective, while a National Archives of Scotland booklet titled *The Scots in America* contains extracts from archive documents and facsimiles of others. I really like these documents, as they provide a direct, first-hand connection with the past. A whole series of these booklets exists and I'll refer to them again with regard to other countries.

With so much interest in genealogy and family history in the US, new researchers can face an almost intimidating amount of information and advice. If you are looking for genealogy websites, especially free-to-use ones, take a look at www.usgenweb.org. Marking its 10th anniversary in 2006, the site was created and is maintained by a dedicated group of volunteers and it is a really useful resource with a multitude of links to follow up. If your interest is more general at this stage – perhaps you just want to find out about your Scottish clan or family name – have a look at Electric Scotland at www.electricscotland.com. Although it is a general Scottish-interest site, its founder has amassed a wealth of information particularly relevant to US researchers. We look at Scottish clans elsewhere in this book, but I do strongly recommend joining your clan or family name association if one exists. They are a fine way of celebrating your Scottish connection in the company of like-minded people. Inevitably, some fellow society members may have ideas about Scottish-ness that you might not agree with, but most members take a more balanced, realistic view of their ancestry and of Scotland's heritage.

The iconic symbol of US immigration heritage is Ellis Island in New York City, where some 12 million immigrants arrived to help build today's America. Information about the Ellis Island museum can be found at www.ellisisland.com. Perhaps of more relevance to ancestral researchers, especially those who cannot visit the museum, is the website of the Statue of Liberty – Ellis Island Foundation, www.ellisisland.org, where you will find inspiration as well as information, including a very useful passenger search facility.

A word of warning about migration from Scotland, though:

"ANCHOR" LINE—AMERICAN MAIL STEAM-SHIPS.

MONEY ORDERS GRANTED ON NEW-YORK FREE OF CHARGE.

"ANCHOR" Line of Steam-Packet Ships, Sailing Regularly
BETWEEN

GLASGOW AND NEW YORK

CARRYING THE UNITED STATES MAIL.

ALEXANDRIA.
ALSATIA.
ANCHORIA.
ANGLIA.
ASSYRIA.
AUSTRALIA.
BOLIVIA.
CALEDONIA.
CALIFORNIA.
CASTALIA.
CIRCASSIA.
COLUMBIA.
DEVONIA.
DORIAN.

ELYSIA.
ETHIOPIA.
INDIA.
ITALIA.
MACEDONIA.
OLYMPIA.
SCANDINAVIA.
SCOTIA.
SIDONIAN.
TRINACRIA.
TYRIAN.
UTOPIA.
VICTORIA.

THESE HIGH-CLASSED POWERFUL CLYDE-BUILT SCREW STEAMSHIPS ARE OFFERED IN THE MOST APPROVED STYLE TO ENSURE THE COMFORT, CONVENIENCE, AND SAFETY OF PASSENGERS, AND ARE INTENDED TO SAIL **FOR NEW-YORK, via MOVILLE.**

"ETHIOPIA,"	-	Thursday, June 19	"ETHIOPIA,"	-	Thursday, July 24	"ETHIOPIA,"	-	Thursday, Aug. 28
"CIRCASSIA,"	-	Thursday, June 26	"CIRCASSIA,"	-	Thursday, July 31	"CIRCASSIA,"	-	Thursday, Sept. 4
"DEVONIA,"	-	Thursday, July 3	"DEVONIA,"	-	Thursday, Aug. 7	"DEVONIA,"	-	Thursday, Sept. 11
"BOLIVIA,"	-	Thursday, July 10	"BOLIVIA,"	-	Thursday, Aug. 14	"BOLIVIA,"	-	Thursday, Sept. 18
"ANCHORIA,"	-	Thursday, July 17	"ANCHORIA,"	-	Thursday, Aug. 21	"ANCHORIA,"	-	Thursday, Sept. 25

PASSENGERS BOOKED TO PHILADELPHIA, BOSTON, QUEBEC, PORTLAND, & BALTIMORE.

RATES OF PASSAGE AND GENERAL REGULATIONS:—

SALOON CABIN—TWELVE, FOURTEEN, and SIXTEEN GUINEAS, according to Accommodation and Situation of Berths, for each Adult. Children from One to Six years of age, are charged at the rate of £7, £10, and £12, per year, and from Six to Twelve years of age, Half-Fare; Infants free. This class of Passengers is found in a Liberal Table, and all accessories, except Wine and Liquors, which can be had on board at Moderate Prices. No Steward's Fee. Return Tickets good for 12 months, Twenty-One, Twenty Three, and Twenty Five Guineas. Five Guineas deposit is required to secure each Berth.

SECOND CABIN.—To New York, Boston, or Philadelphia, Eight Guineas; Children, up to 8 years, Half-Fare; under 1 year, One Guinea. This class of Passengers is provided with Bed, Bedding, &c. Superior Sleeping Berths, and accommodation in Separate Apartments; but other arrangements are the same as Steerage.

STEERAGE.—To New York, Boston, or Philadelphia, Six Guineas. Children, 1 to 8 years, Half-Fare; under 1 year, 1 Guinea. Passengers are provided with Separate Sleeping Berths, but require to provide themselves with Beds and Bedding, a Tin Plate, Quart Mug, Knife, Fork, Spoon, and Water Can, all of which can be hought for 10s. Two Guineas deposit is required to secure each Berth. Daily Water-Can and Lavatory contained is recommended, price 2s 6d. Return Tickets good for 12 months), at lowest current rates.

A liberal supply of Provisions, properly cooked, will be served out by the Company's Servants as follows:—
Breakfast at 8, Dinner at 1, Supper at 6 o'Clock.
No restriction as to QUANTITY will be made so long as no absolute waste is observable.

EACH STEAMER CARRIES A DULY QUALIFIED SURGEON.—NO CHARGE FOR MEDICINES.

LUGGAGE.—SALOON CABIN Passengers are allowed 20 Cubic Feet; Second Cabin, 15 Cubic Feet; Steerage, 10 Cubic Feet of Luggage, the Ship is in no way responsible for its safety. All Luggage must be at Finnieston Quay by Six o'Clock Afternoon of the day previous to Sailing, prominently and legibly addressed, with Owner's Name, Class of Passage, and Name of Ship. No Luggage can be embarked by the River Steamer. Carpet Bags and Small Packages must not be deposited at the Quay, but returned, and taken charge of by the Passengers themselves. Boxes (if required on the voyage) should not exceed Twenty inches in height.

Passengers are particularly Cautioned against Packing up any Merchandise with their Luggage, as it is thereby made Liable to Forfeiture.

PASSAGE-MONEY.—Passengers, by transmitting to the undersigned a Bank or Post-Office Order for amount of the raft required, will have their Berths reserved, and Ticket sent by return of Post. All Balances of Passage Money must be paid by Three o'Clock Afternoon of the day previous to Sailing. Passengers are requested to forward along with the deposit, particulars of Names, Age, Occupation, and Country of Birth of each Person. Infants included. Also, whether Married or Single.

These Steamers are in connection with the ERIE RAILWAY Company from New-York, and form the SHORTEST and most DIRECT ROUTE to the WEST, NORTH, and SOUTH-WESTERN STATES.

Drafts issued on New-York for £1 and upwards free of charge.

LONDON TO NEW YORK, Direct.
EVERY SATURDAY.
FARES.—Saloon Cabin, 11 to 15 Guineas; Steerage, 8 Guineas. Return Tickets on favourable terms.

No Sick, Lame, Deformed, or Infirm Person, or Persons who are in any way liable to become public burdens, can be taken, unless Security is given, as the Subscribers must enter into bonds to the United States and Canadian Governments that such Parties shall not become chargeable to the State.

Certificate of Passage from New-York, Boston, or Philadelphia, issued to Passengers coming to this Country, Steerage, Second Cabin, and Saloon Cabin, at lowest current rates.

THROUGH RATES
Passengers Booked to all Parts of the UNITED STATES and DOMINION OF CANADA at Low Through Rates.
Passengers can also be forwarded to SAN FRANCISCO (CALIFORNIA), CHINA, and JAPAN, by Pacific Railway and Mail Steam-ship Company, at Through Rates.

Apply to HENDERSON BROTHERS, 7 Bowling Green, New-York: 98 Washington Street, Chicago; 34 Leadenhall Street, London: 17 Water Street, Liverpool: 30 Foyle Street, Londonderry: 49 Union Street, Glasgow: or to

J. P. Oliver, 16 Thistle Street, Edinburgh

'Anchor Line' steamships poster.
Reproduced by permission of the Trustees of the
National Library of Scotland.

while Scotland's records of births, marriages and deaths are very comprehensive, there was no requirement on the part of individual emigrants, or those who provided the ships to carry them, to officially record their departure from Scotland. Some ships' passenger lists do survive, but they do not constitute a comprehensive record. Many emigrants from Scotland simply drop out of official records completely at their departure from the homeland. Depending on the date of their emigration and their destination in the US, they may reappear in immigration records in the US but remember, Ellis Island was not the only disembarkation port and, in any case, it was not operational throughout the whole period of Scottish transatlantic emigration. A further difficulty can be the spelling of names, which may have been deliberately or accidentally changed upon arrival. Tracing an unbroken family tree across the Atlantic can be a real challenge.

Most recently, the US has begun celebrating its Scottish heritage with the creation of Tartan Day on April 6, which commemorates the date on which the famous Declaration of Arbroath was signed in 1320. In 1998 the US Senate officially recognised April 6 as 'a celebration of the contribution generations of Scots-Americans have made to the character and prosperity of the United States'. Find out more at www.tartanday.gov.uk and, for details of New York City's week-long celebration look at www.tartanweek.com. As anyone who has been in New York during Tartan Week will tell you, the Scots are well and truly at home then.

Canada

Scotland's connection with Canada is a deep one, and diverse, too. It is different in character, perhaps, depending on which province you are in, with some areas being more aware of the connection than others, but most Scottish families have relatives and friends somewhere in Canada.

Jenni Calder's *Scots in Canada*, the companion volume to the above-mentioned *Scots in the USA*, is a really good read if you want a historical overview of Scottish-Canadian relations. As was the case with the US, the National Archives of Scotland has a booklet on this subject too, *The Scots in Canada*, which presents some important historical documents. I particularly like the extracts from emigrants' letters included in the booklet, as these provide such a personal, often touching, insight into the real human experiences of emigration.

Of many possibilities, there are two particularly good starting points for the new Canadian ancestral researcher. The first is the Library and Archives Canada website at www.collectionscanada.ca. If you follow the link titled *Canadian Genealogy Centre* you will discover 'genealogical content, services, advice, research tools and opportunities to work on joint projects...' Among the excellent resources that are available are a downloadable booklet, *Tracing Your Ancestors in Canada,* and an impressive section on genealogical studies in schools. The second good site for new researchers is www.canadiangenealogy.net, which provides a province-by-province guide to the rich resources that are available.

Canada's Ellis Island, albeit on a smaller scale, is Pier 21, Halifax, Nova Scotia (which literally means 'New Scotland' – where better!), at which around one million people entered the country between 1928 and 1971. You can learn more about this great 20th century series of migrations at Pier 21's well-designed site, www.pier21.ca.

Of course no summary of Canadian resources would be complete without considering the University of Guelph's splendid Scottish Studies Centre: its claim to have been North America's leading centre for Scottish Studies for over 30 years is no empty boast. Ably headed up by Professor Graeme Morton, first ever Chair of Scottish Studies in North America, and supported by the passion, commitment and sheer hard work of the Scottish Studies Foundation, the Centre offers a graduate programme, a range of undergraduate courses and also some distance education courses.

The library at the University of Guelph has one of the largest collections of Scottish material outside Scotland. In October 2005, when Scotland's First Minister visited the University of Guelph, I was lucky enough to participate too. While the First Minister talked to students and the assembled press, and looked at some of the archival treasures, the archivist quietly invited me to have a behind-the-scenes look at the full Scottish collection. We slipped away, a pair of archival conspirators, and I enjoyed a quick tour of this most impressive collection. For more on the Scottish Studies Centre look at www.uoguelph.ca/scottish, and for more on the Foundation, visit www.scottishstudies.com. Proving that Scottish connections extend all the way across Canada, the University of Victoria, British Columbia also recently announced the appointment of its first-ever Scottish Studies Fellow and Simon Fraser University's Centre for Scottish Studies was established in 1999.

To reinforce my point about the depth of the Scottish connection in Canada generally but particularly in Guelph, I'd like to share my experience of giving a presentation at the University. The First Minister and the following speaker, Professor Tom Devine, having made their speeches and departed to catch flights back across the Atlantic, I was left to take the stage and talk about Scottish connections with Canada. To begin the presentation I asked the audience

'Anchor Line' accompanying map of the United States and Canada.
Reproduced by permission of the Trustees of the
National Library of Scotland.

– some 250 people – to raise their hands if they had a personal connection with Scotland. The whole roomful of people proudly raised their hands.

New Zealand

New Zealand was discovered by European sailors in the 17th century but it was not explored until the first of Captain James Cook's expeditions in 1769. Numbers of emigrants there were not large until the 19th century when communications improved and more land became available for settlement. Scottish migration to New Zealand was extensive, especially from the 1840s onwards. It has been said, indeed, that at one time up to a quarter of immigrants in New Zealand were of Scots ancestry. Dunedin claims to be the most Scottish city in New Zealand – small wonder, as its moniker is an Anglicisation of the Gaelic name for Scotland's capital city, Edinburgh.

A selection of interesting background historical documents can be found in the National Archives of Scotland booklet, *The Scots in New Zealand*. Reading primary historical documents of this kind is a great way to bring the history books to life. Once you are ready to begin researching your own ancestry, though, the Archives New Zealand website at www.archives.govt.nz is perhaps the best starting point. Archives New Zealand describes itself as 'the memory of government', which is a thoughtful, positive way to express the role.

There are two segments of the Archives New Zealand site of special interest to ancestral researchers. The first is a clear and comprehensive, downloadable family history reference guide. The second is an online search facility called *Archway* which provides access to records including births, marriages and deaths, education, migration, citizenship and war records. This is an impressive and enormously useful collection of resources.

For sports fans, Scotland's ancestral connections with New Zealand have at least one important benefit today: Scotland's rugby selectors have been able to tap into some of New Zealand's considerable rugby talent and bring some of Scotland's sons home to play for their ancestral national team – Tartan All Blacks, perhaps, or Kilted Kiwis as they are better known?

Australia

The early years of European settlement in Australia were dominated by the use of the continent as a penal colony – a destination for transported criminals – and the first convict ship arrived there in 1788. Fortunately, Scottish convicts were only a small proportion of the total number of criminals transported to Australia. With the passage of time, increasing numbers of free settlers arrived down under and the country today is a vibrant and multicultural society with a positive outlook.

There are two excellent starting points for ancestral researchers in Australia. The first is the National Library of Australia, www.nla.gov.au. The family history section of this site lists the major resources held in the library and provides a most useful set of links to other resources. The alternative place to start, also an official one, is the National Archives of Australia, www.naa.gov.au. Like the National Library site, there is a lot of useful information and advice and the site makes it very clear what information is and is not available, and how and where to obtain it. I particularly like the 'Making Australia Home' service which, for a fee, can provide migrants and their descendants with copies of relevant records in a presentation pack.

As for Scottish connections to Australia, the National Archives of Scotland's booklet *The Scots in Australia*, part of a series covering all the main 'diaspora' countries, will help you understand the historical background and introduce you to some fascinating historical documents.

One other Scottish resource of special relevance to Australia deserves mention. Between 1852 and 1857, the Highlands and Islands Emigration Society helped about 5,000 people emigrate to

Australia from this impoverished region of Scotland. An index to these passenger lists is available at www.scan.org.uk, together with a lot of fascinating background material, including an 1852 newspaper account of a mutiny on board one of the emigrant ships.

England and Wales

It may seem a little strange including England and Wales in a discussion of countries affected by the Scottish Diaspora. After all, they all lie together on the same island, and they are all technically part of the same country, Great Britain. However, many Scots did move south, especially during the Industrial Revolution, and very real differences exist between the nations of Great Britain – the Scottish legal system is different to the English system, for example; many government records are held separately; and Scotland now has its own Parliament. (Wales also has its own Assembly, but its powers are not as extensive as those given to the Scottish Parliament.)

For people starting their ancestral research in England and Wales, the resources available are often different. I'd like to draw attention to just four resources here. First, Genuki, which we have already identified as a Scottish resource, also includes information on England, Wales and indeed Ireland. While it is a wonderful resource, don't forget that this website was created and is maintained by volunteers so you should double-check that any information you plan to use from it is accurate and up-to-date.

Second, have a look at the National Archives website at www.nationalarchives.gov.uk. Scotland has its own archives, as we have seen, but you may find a lot of useful information here as well. For example, there is online access to the service registers of Royal Navy seamen who joined the Service between 1873 and 1923, so if one of your ancestors was in the Royal Navy, you may find them here.

Third, the Origins Network at www.originsnetwork.com is a very comprehensive, professionally presented website for genealogists. There are free name and place searches to get you started, but the bulk of the information is only available on a subscription basis. If you are going to do a lot of research, however, this might make a good investment.

Finally, again if you are undertaking research on a serious basis, you should consider joining the Society of Genealogists, a registered charity whose members have as their focus 'the study, science and knowledge of genealogy'. The Society's large library is available to members and there are regular lectures and courses. Have a look at www.sog.org.uk for more about the society and its membership.

If you are in England or Wales, a visit to Scotland is easy and very worthwhile. Doing Scottish ancestral research online is relatively straightforward but doing research in person in Scotland can be an inspirational experience, even if included as just part of a short weekend break.

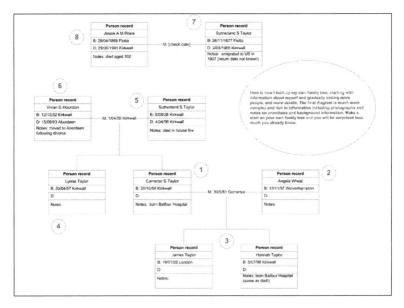

There are many different family tree diagrams in use and special software available. The illustration here shows one of the author's own diagrams at an early stage in his research, showing the order in which the family tree was created.

Ireland

By 'Ireland', I refer mainly to Northern Ireland rather than to the Republic of Ireland, and by Northern Ireland I really mean the Province of Ulster, which was heavily settled by Scottish migrants. These migrants have become known variously as the Ulster-Scots, the Scots-Irish or even the Scotch-Irish, the latter terms used mainly in North America where so many Ulster-Scots eventually settled. In the next chapter, The Ulster Connection, we will look more closely at this unique group of emigrants.

Getting Going with Your Research

As you have seen, there are many routes to finding your roots and we have only really scratched the surface of the resources available to you. There is no single 'right' way to travel on your ancestral journey but there are some broad principles that are worth reflecting on here. First, start from what you know and work backwards in time – travel from the known to the unknown. By doing so, you will ensure that your research will be built on a secure foundation of accurate knowledge. Secondly, official sources of information are generally more accurate than unofficial ones: even if you don't use original, official records in the first instance of your research, double-check everything that you learn against them whenever you have the opportunity. Don't make assumptions or use guesswork which can't subsequently be tested, or you risk leaving inaccuracies and misinformation for future generations of your family.

Third, use the various routes to roots in whatever order you wish. It is *your* ancestry that you are exploring and you should do so in your own way and at your own pace. Fourth, keep a record of your journey of discovery for future reference. Write everything down, perhaps in a single journal so that everything is in one place. (Some people chose to do this as a diary.)

Finally, mix your research with actual physical journeys to places that are connected with your ancestors or where you can find additional resources to research them further, perhaps sources that will help you understand the lives and times of your ancestors, not just the basic information such as births, marriages and deaths. As you'll see in the next chapter, doing so can transform your understanding of their lives and perhaps even give deeper meaning to your own.

CHAPTER 4

The Ulster Connection

WHEN I ARRIVED IN BELFAST to begin my own investigation into the Ulster-Scots, the taxi driver who took me from the airport to my hotel wanted to know where I'd come from. 'Ah, Scotland' he said, 'sure, my mother's family was Scottish, you know. A long time ago, mind, but we still go there on holiday. It's a grand place'. He then asked what brought me to Belfast and I explained that I was doing some research for a book and wanted to discover how people could explore their Ulster-Scots ancestry. 'Oh, we get a lot of them', my driver replied. I took that as a good omen and regarded my journey as duly justified.

Ulster, for the uninitiated, is one of the four Provinces of Ireland. Six of Ulster's nine counties now form Northern Ireland, and the remaining three counties of the historical Province of Ulster lie in the Republic of Ireland. Belfast (which, in an interesting reinforcement of the Scottish-US connections, it twinned with Nashville, Tennessee) is the principal city and administrative centre of Northern Ireland.

Scotland and Ulster are of course close neighbours – only fifteen miles separate them at their closest point – and for our seagoing ancestors there was little difficulty in travelling from one to the other. Connections between the two areas go back hundreds and hundreds of years, but it is really the last 400 or so years that interest us here. A distinctive group of people known as the Ulster-Scots emerged in the first half of this period, only to be submerged for a time during the latter half. Today we find ourselves amidst a reawakening of Ulster-Scots consciousness.

The Ulster-Scots are known in the US as the Scotch-Irish or Scots-Irish. They are often seen as part of the Irish diaspora, but

Scotland doesn't give up its sons and daughters lightly and this group can be regarded as part of Scotland's history too, though they are a relatively little known part of it.

In this chapter we will look at the historical background to the Ulster-Scots and consider their impact, mainly in the US, through their migrations in the 17th and 18th centuries. Did you know, for example, that seventeen American presidents are believed to have Ulster ancestry? Other famous names include storyteller Mark Twain (the pen name of Samuel Langhorne Clemens), Davy Crockett – hero of the Alamo – and Alexander Turney Stewart, an Ulster-born entrepreneur who became one of the richest Americans of all time. My Belfast taxi driver had the last word, however. Could I guess, he asked, the name of a famous female singer with Ulster-Scot ancestry? I tried but quickly admitted defeat. 'Dolly Parton!' he said triumphantly as we arrived at my hotel.

Historical Background

I spent my first evening in Belfast reading about the history of Ulster. Background reading is always useful at the start of any new research because it sets a wider context and can suggest useful avenues for further exploration. Here is what I discovered.

English (and later, British) involvement in Irish affairs goes back to the Middle Ages. The early histories of England, Wales, Scotland and Ireland are intertwined to such an extent that you cannot treat the story of any part of today's United Kingdom in isolation. The real starting point for my exploration of the Ulster connection begins in 1603.

1603

In March 1603, Queen Elizabeth of England died childless, having ruled for 44 years. On her deathbed, she declared King James VI of Scotland as her heir, and with these words the last Tudor monarch made way for the Stuart dynasty. James VI was the only son of

Elizabeth's cousin, Mary Queen of Scots, whom Elizabeth had had executed after finding Mary guilty of plotting to assassinate and overthrow her. Upon his coronation, the crowns of England and Scotland were united and the two nations brought together under a sole monarch.

At the time of her death, Queen Elizabeth was close to defeating Hugh O'Neill, Earl of Tyrone, in Ulster, a rebel whose Spanish allies had landed at Kinsale in 1601 but were forced to surrender to English forces the following year. Elizabeth was never to have the satisfaction of accepting O'Neill's surrender, though negotiations were under way at the time of her death. After many years of warfare, Ulster was the last Irish Province to be brought under the control of the English (and now Scottish) Crown.

King James VI of Scotland now found himself as King James I of England, Scotland, Ireland and, so he claimed, France (though his ambitions regarding France were never realised). The Province of Ulster was devastated from years of warfare and the King and his advisers turned their attentions towards efforts of reconstruction. Here we begin to see the first glimmerings of the dawn of the Ulster-Scots.

The Hamilton and Montgomery Settlement

It is said that the Lowlands of Scotland were overpopulated at the beginning of the 17th century. Landowners and entrepreneurs in Ayrshire, in the west of Scotland, must have looked across the short stretch of water separating Scotland and Ulster and wondered what opportunities might exist there now that the Province had been brought under control.

Two such men were James Hamilton and Hugh Montgomery, both of whom were born in Ayrshire and had access to the Royal Court. Opportunity arose for them due to the imprisonment of one Con O'Neill, an Irish chieftain with landholdings in the east of Ulster who was arrested on charges of treason. Fortunately for O'Neill, Queen Elizabeth's death delayed his execution, and the extra time allowed his resourceful wife to come up with a plan for his escape.

With her husband lying imprisoned in Carrickfergus Castle, north of Belfast, Con O'Neill's wife suggested a bold strategy to Hugh Montgomery. If Montgomery could free O'Neill and gain for him a Royal Pardon, the O'Neill's would give Montgomery half of their lands in Ulster as a reward. A risky, if profitable, plan, Montgomery duly engineered the escape of O'Neill and brought the fugitive to his home in Ayrshire.

All was well until James Hamilton discovered the plan and intervened in order to secure advantage for himself, persuading King James I to divide the O'Neill lands into three portions, not two. O'Neill received a pardon and retained one-third of his lands, Hugh Montgomery received one-third and James Hamilton the remaining third, at which Montgomery must have been absolutely furious. Historians describe the resulting settlements in County Antrim and County Down as the Hamilton and Montgomery Settlement, but there can surely have been little co-operation between the two men as they re-housed their tenants from Ayrshire in these areas: each would have regarded the other as a rival.

In 1606 the first of some 10,000 settlers began to arrive in Ulster by boat from Scotland. Much like the later opening up of the American frontier, the settlers had an enormous impact on the devastated lands they found. The settlement was successful and quickly spread beyond its initial boundaries, as the predominantly Protestant Scottish settlers sought new land and new opportunities in the area. Arguably, the efforts of Hamilton and Montgomery created Scotland's first overseas colony, and this success encouraged King James to create three further plantations: Virginia in 1607, the west of Ulster in 1610, and Nova Scotia in 1621.

An excellent website – www.HamiltonMontgomery1606.com – with supporting printed materials including a leaflet, a map and a fascinating CD-ROM containing original manuscripts, was created in 2006 to commemorate the 400th anniversary of the Hamilton and Montgomery Settlement.

The Ulster Plantation

In 1607 two leading Irish Earls – Hugh O'Neill, Earl of Tyrone (whom we met previously) and Rory O'Donnell, Earl of Tyrconnell – left Ireland for Spain, in the company of a number of family members and followers, to seek support there for further rebellion against the English. Forced by bad weather to land in France and having to travel overland from there to Rome, they were destined never to return to Ireland. This incident, referred to as the Flight of the Earls, left the way clear for the King to confiscate all of their lands in Ulster.

King James I was determined to plant loyal settlers in the con-fiscated lands to ensure that they remained under his control. The royal intention was to create concentrations of settlers in and around towns and garrisons, establishing well defended, loyal communities of English and Scottish Protestants in order to permanently subdue the Catholic Irish. The first of these 'planted' settlers arrived in 1610.

The reality of the plantation, of course, did not go as originally planned, not least because those in charge of the plantation found it difficult to recruit English settlers. This led to the dominance of Lowland Scots in the plantation settlements, Highland Scots being discouraged from the Ulster settlements because of concerns that they might have too much sympathy with the Gaelic-speaking Irish, with whom they had had contact for generations. Overall, however, the plantation was successful and by 1630 the total population of settlers may have numbered 80,000.

The middle of the 17th century was a turbulent time in England, Scotland and Ireland. Some of the original settlers chose to return to Scotland, while a further wave of Scottish migration, fuelled by famine in the Lowlands, took place in the 1690s. Religious differ-ences became more apparent as Presbyterianism became the dom-inant religion in Ulster, though the Presbyterians found themselves excluded from political power and influence.

Religious intolerance and economic factors led to a trickle of migration across the Atlantic in the 17th century, but with the linen industry-fuelled growth of the Ulster economy some way off, and greater religious freedoms being sought, pressure was mounting for a major population movement westwards across the sea.

The First Wave of Transatlantic Migration

Historians argue about whether economic or religious reasons were the principal cause of the migrations of Ulster-Scots in the 18th century, but the reality is likely to be a mix of the two. A desire for adventure on the part of some of the more hardy spirits among the migrants was also likely a contributing factor; this was probably encouraged by friends and relations already in North America. Religion also had a strong part to play, as the vast majority of the 18th century migrants were Protestants, many of them Presbyterians.

The first of five great waves of organised emigration in the century took place in 1718 when perhaps five or six ships sailed from Londonderry and Coleraine in Ulster bound for Boston. Record-keeping at the time being patchy, we cannot be absolutely certain of the number of ships nor the number of passengers. These initial settlers spread out around Maine, New Hampshire (where they founded a new Londonderry) and Massachusetts, no doubt delighted to make landfall after their arduous six to eight week transatlantic sea voyage. By comparison, today a transatlantic flight is typically six to eight *hours*.

A fascinating website, www.1718migration.org.uk, has been created by the Ulster Scots Agency in association with the Ulster Historical Foundation, the Centre for Migration Studies and the Institute of Ulster-Scots Studies providing more information about the 1718 migration.

Flood Tide and Beyond

This first migration was the start of a series of waves that brought an estimated quarter of a million people from Ulster to America over the course of the rest of the 18th century. Successive waves took place in 1725–29, 1740–41, 1754–55 and 1771–75, with migrants settling in the eastern US in the early years. Later, as land became scarcer along the Eastern Seaboard and opportunity beckoned further inland, the Ulster-Scots moved westwards into frontier territories. Ulster connections have been described as at their deepest in the Shenandoah Valley of Virginia and East Tennessee, and in western Pennsylvania; however, New Hampshire, West Virginia, eastern and central Tennessee, North Carolina, the South Carolina Piedmont, Kentucky, North Georgia, Alabama and parts of Texas are also important areas in terms of Ulster-Scots settlement.

In the 19th century the character of emigration from Ireland changed and people of all denominations, from all regions of Ireland, became involved. Particularly significant was the mass migration caused by the Great Famine of 1845–49.

The extent of the Ulster-Scots' involvement in the Irish diaspora to the US was a surprise – of the 44 million or so people in America who claim Irish ancestry, an estimated 56 per cent can trace their roots back to the 18th century Ulster emigrations. What, then, was the impact of this migration?

The Impact of Ulster-Scots Migrants

If you are one of the 22 million or so Americans with Ulster-Scots roots, you are in good company. For a start, 17 US Presidents have been of Ulster-Scots ancestry. The first was Andrew Jackson, the seventh American President (1829–37) and the founder of the Democratic Party; the most recent is George W. Bush (2001–). Some of the Ulster-Scots presidential connections are more direct than others, but 17 out of 43 Presidents represents quite a record of achievement.

Emigrants from Ulster had an immediate impact on the emerging US nation. They were resourceful, confident people, used to hard work in frontier conditions. Their pioneering spirit saw them at the vanguard of westwards expansion, creating a new country where ideas of freedom and independence came to be enshrined in the Constitution. Many Ulster-Scots were American patriots and several played important parts in the framing of the Declaration of Independence, which was signed on 4 July 1776. George Washington paid tribute to the ideals of freedom held by the Ulster-Scots when he reportedly said that 'if defeated everywhere else I will make my last stand for liberty among the Scotch-Irish of my native Virginia.'

In religion, too, the Presbyterian Ulster-Scots had an impact on the growing nation. The Reverend Francis Makemie, Moderator of the first American Presbytery, formed in 1706, would have been proud of the achievements of his successors who established Presbyterianism as the second-largest denomination in America by the time of the Declaration of Independence.

The roll-call of Ulster-Scots contributors to American history is a long one, and there is space for only a few names here:

Davy Crockett, the proverbial 'King of the Wild Frontier' and the hero of the Alamo, had his roots in Ulster; his parents were Ulster-Scots emigrants.

One half of the Lewis and Clark partnership that explored the American west as far as the Pacific at the start of the 19th century, opening up the continent for settlement, was Ulster-Scots: William Clark was of emigrant stock.

Thomas Andrew Mellon, an extremely successful business-man in 19th century America, emigrated from Ulster as a child. His story is told at the Ulster American Folk Park near Omagh in Northern Ireland – to which we will return later.

In literature, Ulster can lay claim to the ancestors of the author Samuel Langhorne Clemens, better known to us under the pseudonym Mark Twain.

The strong music and dance traditions the emigrants took with them on their travels are noted by Billy Kennedy, a prolific author on the Ulster-Scots in America, in his book *Our Most Priceless Heritage*:

The distinctive styles of many modern-day American country, bluegrass and folk music performers can be traced directly back to the 18th century Ulster-Scots...

Small wonder then, that two such well-known country singers as Dolly Parton and Ricky Skaggs can claim Ulster-Scots ancestry.

Lest we are left with the impression that Ulster-Scots only had an impact on the US, three further individuals are worth highlighting. The first two are John Balance and William Ferguson Massey, Prime Ministers of New Zealand – Balance from 1891 to 1893 and Massey from 1912 to 1925 – both of whom were Ulster-Scots emigrants.

In Canada, we can point to one very well-known figure, Timothy Eaton. Eaton emigrated from Ulster as a young man and went on to build a Canadian business empire founded on department stores – the first Eaton's was in Yonge Street, Toronto – and the then-revolutionary concept of mail order. Eaton's became a household name in Canada, and the Eaton Centre in Toronto remains the city's largest shopping centre.

The list of influential Ulster-Scots who have made contributions around the globe goes on and on. The Internet is a wonderful source of such information and is worth exploring if you have the time and inclination; for now, though, I'd like to turn to your own Ulster-Scots connections and how they can be explored.

Making Connections

My own visit to Belfast was all about making connections – meeting people, discovering information and getting an understanding of how you can get started tracing your Ulster-Scots ancestry. As I mentioned earlier, one of the themes of this book is that to truly understand your ancestral heritage, you need to visit the places your ancestors knew.

The Ulster American Folk Park

www.folkpark.com

I began my visit to Northern Ireland by visiting the Ulster American Folk Park. Opened in 1976, the Folk Park is an outdoor museum telling the story of the two million or so people who left Ulster between 1700 and 1900, the majority of them bound for North America. The Park is located near the town of Omagh in County Tyrone and is run by MAGNI, the Museums and Galleries of Northern Ireland.

A new permanent indoor exhibition called *Emigrants* explores themes such as People and Places, Failure and Opportunity, and Survival and Prosperity. I recommend taking time to read the exhibition material carefully as it sets out the background to emigration from Ireland very well and prepares you for the outdoor exhibition. Look out for the explanatory leaflet too, which guides you around the outdoor exhibition.

The outdoor exhibition consists of thirty buildings linked by a path, with an accompanying printed map and guide. Costumed interpreters can be found in the main buildings along the way and it is worth talking to them; they are relaxed, friendly, informative and they bring the exhibit buildings to life in a charming, engaging way.

The first part of the outdoor museum is the Old World area, showing the buildings and ways of life of Ulster in the 18th and 19th centuries. Some of the buildings have been rebuilt here while others are reconstructions. Of particular interest is the Mellon Homestead, the birthplace of Thomas Mellon, who went on to emigrate and achieve remarkable financial success in America.

Halfway through the museum, the mood changes and you walk down a reconstruction of a 19th century Ulster street which ends at the dockside. There, you find a full-scale replica of the brig *Union*, an emigrant sailing ship that you board in order to hear about the conditions that emigrants experienced during their journey abroad.

Emerging from the other side of the ship, you find yourself in a 19th century American street as you step ashore in the New World. The effect is extraordinary and very emotionally charged for visitors with emigrant ancestry.

One of the reconstructed buildings on this street is the First Mellon Bank, a symbol of the success of the Mellon family's migration and which provides good contrast to the way the Mellon family lived in Ulster. Moving on through the exhibit, you find yourself apparently travelling westwards through Pennsylvania, admiring the skills of the settlers who created farmland and homes from wilderness.

Guided by the map and leaflet, you will eventually return to the main museum building. The experience of visiting the Ulster American Folk Park as a whole is hugely rewarding and is a really good way to attain deeper understanding of the reasons behind, and the experience of, migration from Ulster. Don't miss the opportunity to visit the Folk Park as part of your own journey of discovery. In particular, special events and celebrations, including annual American Independence Celebrations in July and the internationally famous Appalachian and Bluegrass Music Festival in September, are worth attending.

The Centre for Migration Studies

www.qub.ac.uk/cms/

Just beside the Folk Park is the Centre for Migration Studies (CMS), my next port of call. The Centre was established in its present form in 1998 and it combines a number of different resources under one roof. As well as being an academic institution, the CMS is also a public library with an impressive collection of books relating to migration topics. It is also responsible for the Irish Emigration Database Project and has custody of a most useful database of emigration related records, including copies of emigration letters and journals.

Reconstructed settler house at the Ulster American Folk Park near Omagh, Northern Ireland.

© Seabridge Consultants.

Visitors to the Centre, many of whom have their interest stimulated by a tour of the Folk Park, can search the database, which is also available at the Public Record Office in Belfast (though it is not, as yet, available via the Internet). Transcription and input of documents has been underway for 17 years with a resulting wealth of information in the database.

The Centre, which is free to use (with the exception of photocopying), handles countless enquiries, over half of which are Ulster-Scots-related, so the friendly, highly motivated staff there have built up a great deal of knowledge and expertise in Ulster-Scots migration research. The Centre staff see migration as an ongoing contemporary phenomenon, something that touches all of us. Levels of migration into western Europe from other parts of the world, including the countries in eastern Europe which have recently joined the European Union, are considerable and the Centre's staff suggests that a better understanding of our ancestors' migration will help us welcome today's immigrants.

The CMS sees itself as part of a dynamic network of people and organisations trying to meet the needs of ancestral tourists. While a visit is certainly enjoyable, you should bear in mind that the focus of the Centre's work is the wider emigration context and it can provide only limited assistance with research into specific families, though you can search for names in the emigration database. For more detailed research you must turn to the resources of the Public Record Office and the Ulster Historical Foundation. Returning to Belfast that evening, therefore, I made arrangements to visit them both.

The Public Record Office of Northern Ireland

www.proni.gov.uk

The next day, I accordingly went to the Public Record Office of Northern Ireland, referred to as PRONI (pronounced *pro-knee*.) PRONI houses records produced by central and local government in Northern Ireland, and records and papers that belonged to a number of private individuals. Note that PRONI does not hold birth, marriage or death certificates – these are held at the General Register Office elsewhere in Belfast. A myth about Irish ancestral research is that all of the relevant records were destroyed in a fire in 1922. While it is true that many records were indeed destroyed, much useful information still exists at PRONI, and elsewhere.

The Public Record Office is situated in Balmoral Avenue, just a taxi-ride from the town centre, and visitors enter via a functional security building that belies the welcoming and helpful staff inside the Record Office itself. A very efficient receptionist quickly established that I was a first-time visitor, issued me with a pass and directed me to a 'new arrivals' seating area just inside the main office. Shortly a member of staff came over to me, introduced himself, and described the Record Office's collection and facilities, and asked what my particular interest was – a brilliant service for first-time visitors. Having discovered the reason for my visit – research for this book – a supervisor was quickly summoned and I was given a fascinating insight into PRONI's work and its collections.

The most important piece of preparation before you visit PRONI, as anywhere, is always to do your homework thoroughly beforehand and identify as many personal and place names as possible that you wish to research while at the site. This combination of personal *and* place names is particularly important in Ulster research.

The counties in Ireland are subdivided administratively in a unique way. Counties are divided into 'baronies', which in turn are divided into parishes. Parishes are further subdivided into 'townlands', a land division with very ancient roots that bears no relationship to towns in the modern sense. There are about 62,000 townlands in Ireland used in official record-keeping. To embark on Ulster ancestral research with any real prospect of success, then, you will need the combination of personal name and of townland. Otherwise, the official records may be terribly difficult to use and you may begin making assumptions about whether someone was or was not your ancestor. As we have already discussed, unverified assumptions are not a suitable basis for ancestral research.

Armed with as much information as possible before you arrive, you are ready to search the Personal Names Card-Index, the Householders Index and the computerised Geographical Index. Each of these provides a starting point, enabling you to identify potentially useful documents which you can then study in detail. Some records are available online, some are on microfilm and others can only be studied in their original hard-copy form. Records that ancestral researchers will find particularly useful include street directories, the 1901 census, Griffith's Valuation (1856–1865), wills, school records and workhouse admission records.

In all, the Public Record Office has about 53 kilometres of shelves packed with records. The PRONI website contains much good advice and essential information, and there is a large collection of information sheets in the search rooms at the Record Office itself. PRONI's friendly, knowledgeable staff are there to help and guide you and their service is free, so the Record Office is your best starting point in Belfast for researching your Ulster-Scots ancestry. The staff will not undertake genealogical research for you, however: if you require that sort of service then you will need to commission a professional researcher.

The Ulster Historical Foundation

www.ancestryireland.com

Having satisfied my curiosity about the Public Record Office, I returned to central Belfast to visit the Ulster Historical Foundation's premises. Established in 1956, the Foundation is an educational charity with a focus on Irish and Ulster-Scots ancestral research.

The Foundation's attractive, informative website is a very useful resource for ancestral researchers. Joining the membership association of the Foundation gives you access to online searchable databases, enabling you to make progress with your research before visiting Ulster in person. In addition, the Foundation offers a comprehensive and professional research service, undertaken by its own highly experienced research team. It is rightly described as the premier genealogical research agency in Northern Ireland.

I met with Dr William Roulston, the Ulster Historical Foundation's Research Officer. His book, *Researching Scots-Irish Ancestors*, is the definitive genealogical guide to early modern Ulster from 1600–1800, the key period for Scottish settlement in Ulster and the onward migration of so many Ulster-Scots. If you are intending to embark on Ulster-Scots ancestral research, I strongly recommend that you acquire a copy. The Foundation also publishes a wide range of other quality books covering Irish genealogy and history topics, and has a strong commitment to outreach, including in North America, so keep an eye on its website for details of upcoming events.

Professional Genealogists Revisited

www.apgi.ie

As always, engaging the services of a professional genealogist can be a good way to get your research done if you do not have the time to undertake it yourself. Professional research does come at a price, however, and you should select your researcher carefully, seeking references or other evidence of ability. The Public Record Office will be able to provide you with a list of researchers, but you must remember that PRONI cannot provide recommendations.

Many researchers are members of the Association of Professional Genealogists in Ireland, a regulating body committed to achieving high standards amongst its members. More information and a list of members can be found at its website, www.apgi.ie.

General Register Office

www.groni.gov.uk

The General Register Office (Northern Ireland) is the governmental body responsible for the administration of marriage law and for civil registration of births, deaths, marriages and adoptions in Northern Ireland. It has registers of marriages from 1845 onwards and registers of births and deaths dating from 1864.

In line with the principle that nothing in ancestral research is ever completely straightforward, these records are held in different places. In the main General Register Office at Oxford House in the centre of Belfast, you will find birth and death registers from 1864 onwards and marriage registers from 1922 onwards. For marriage registers dating from April 1845 for non-Catholic marriages and January 1864 for all other marriages, you will have to look in District Registrars' offices

While this is all very confusing, the General Register Office's website does its best to make the situation clearer and to point you in the right direction. There are public search facilities at the main office in Belfast where, for a fee, you can search the computer indexes. While the office does not carry out genealogical research on your behalf, you can pay for what is termed an 'assisted search', where a member of staff will work with you. This is a good option, especially if you are short of time.

North of Ireland Family History Society (NIFHS)

www.nifhs.org

It is always a good idea to join the Family History Society that covers your geographic area of interest, and the North of Ireland Family History Society is no exception. NIFHS has a number of branches and also offers associate membership. It is not a research agency, but you will get lots of support and encouragement from fellow members and you may find people working on ancestral research that overlaps your own. The Society has a library at its premises in Belfast, with an excellent collection of reference books and journals. There is more information about the Society, including contact details, at its website, www.nifhs.org.

The Ulster-Scots Agency

www.ulsterscotsagency.com

My expedition to Belfast ended with a visit to the Ulster-Scots Agency. The Agency is a cross-border government body, one of six such organisations established following the Good Friday peace agreement. It has a responsibility to promote the Ulster-Scots language – recognised as a regional language under the European Charter for Regional and Minority Languages – and also Ulster-Scots culture in general: a challenging remit, but the Agency has set to it with a real will. There are some critics who dispute the need for Ulster-Scots descendants to assert such a strong sense of identity, particularly when the Ulster-Scots diaspora was assimilated so early – and so thoroughly – in North America, but the Agency has no such doubts and has busied itself funding other bodies and carrying out some activities directly. The Hamilton and Montgomery Settlement and 1718 Migration websites and associated leaflets mentioned earlier in this chapter were produced by the Ulster-Scots Agency, together with an impressive – both in terms of quality and number – range of leaflets, a map and CD, among other items.

There is a close relationship, naturally, between Scotland's heritage and that of the Ulster-Scots, thus the Agency is committed to joint working wherever it is possible to do so, for example with local government agencies in the southwest of Scotland from whence many Ulster-Scots emigrated. This effort is bound to benefit ancestral researchers, as it will draw attention to the depth and importance of the connections and the resources that are available to assist researchers. In carrying out its remit, the Ulster-Scots Agency is promoting Northern Ireland as a place that is aware of its diverse heritage and wants to share it with visitors. Ulster-Scots culture, the Agency would argue, is alive and well. Do visit the Agency's website at www.ulsterscotsagency.com if you wish to learn more about its activities.

During my visit to Belfast, I was struck by the way people talked about migration: they saw it as a fact of life, not just something that happened in the past but that goes on today and touches all of us. There was a strong sense of a need for understanding, for by understanding the past we are better able to understand our present and plan for the future. Few can argue with such a sentiment.

The Northern Ireland Tourism Board and its partners in Ireland recognise the importance of the Ulster-Scots connection and are keen to welcome ancestral researchers back home, whether undertaking detailed research or simply exploring the places that their ancestors lived and worked. Based on my own experience, I encourage anyone with Ulster-Scots ancestry to explore it in depth. You never know, you may be related to Davy Crockett, an American President or two, or you might even – and this would make my Belfast taxi driver friend very happy – share an ancestor with Dolly Parton!

CHAPTER 5

Touching the Past

HUMANS HAVE ALWAYS TRAVELLED, whether it has been in search of food and water or simply to discover new places. We are a species blessed – or cursed, depending on your perspective – with insatiable curiosity. Archaeologists and anthropologists generally agree that early humans spread out of Africa in a series of waves, colonising new parts of our world as the climate changed and landscapes and habitats were transformed. Our earliest human ancestors were hunters and gatherers who would have moved to follow their food supply – after all, humans are not the only species that migrates. The advent of farming enabled the creation of larger, static settlements where land could be cultivated, crops grown and permanent homes built. Nevertheless, our human curiosity and expanding population kept us on the move, discovering new landscapes, fresh opportunities and challenges. We do not know how these people in our past thought or what they felt, but we can imagine that they retained some sense of where they came from as they travelled onwards. Perhaps the idea of home and the reality of homeland are as old as mankind as a species.

Generation after generation, as the first settled farming communities were established and towns and cities grew and multiplied, we have migrated from place to place to shape the world in which we now live. From these movements of individuals, and sometimes whole communities, away from the known, comes our sense of connection with the places of our past. Your sense of connection with Scotland, that feeling of rootedness, is one of the principal themes of this book; another is that, in order to truly understand the past, you need to see and touch it in order to really know it. In other words, you need to embark on an ancestral journey, taking you to a place that you know or discover is home: the place where your family roots are deepest.

Homecomings of this kind, whether undertaken on an individual basis or as part of a group, are what this chapter is all about. I hope that it will help you understand why touching the past is important to your sense of identity, both as an individual and as a member of an extended family sharing common ancestors. Few people who have undertaken an ancestral journey of this sort would regard it as 'just' tourism. Understanding this has been a very real challenge for tourism agencies and we will look first of all at how Scotland's national tourism agency has responded to the challenges and opportunities of what is commonly referred to as 'ancestral tourism'.

Ancestral Tourism in Scotland

Genealogy and family history have always interested and intrigued people, but the past twenty years or so – perhaps even a little longer – have seen an astonishing rise in the popularity of these subjects. More and more ancestral resources have become available over the past few decades, though whether this has been a cause or a consequence of this rise in the popularity of ancestral research is an interesting question.

The work of the Mormons has been of vital importance in making ancestral research sources available, as has the rapid development of the Internet, which has enabled us to access information via the World Wide Web and to communicate with each other, wherever we are, quickly and easily via the Internet. The General Register Office for Scotland and the National Archives of Scotland were quick to see the potential of the Internet and, as a result, their success in making primary research material available in digital form has enabled Scotland to become a world leader in this field.

Accompanying the increasing popularity of genealogy and family history, more and more people with Scottish ancestry are making the journey back home to Scotland. There is an increasing awareness these days of the importance of roots, of connections with a homeland. This became especially noticeable in the late 1990s as the last century drew to a close and the 21st century – once the stuff of science fiction – beckoned. The significance of the new Millennium influenced many people's thoughts regarding their own and their family's place in history, giving them a sense of belonging and of being part of something bigger.

The Welsh Tourist Board certainly recognised this link between the Millennium and peoples' thoughts and feelings about an ancestral homeland, mounting a Millennium marketing campaign aimed at the Welsh diaspora. People of Welsh ancestry were invited to return during a year-long homecoming. The response of the Scottish Executive and tourism agencies in Scotland was more restrained, but has arguably been more successful in the long term.

In its *New Strategy for Scottish Tourism*, published in 2000, the Scottish Executive identified 'genealogy tourism' as a phenomenon worth exploring further, though it quickly became apparent that a broader definition was needed and the term 'ancestral tourism' came into use. In its initial research, VisitScotland – the national tourism agency – realised that increasing numbers of people from abroad were indeed researching their ancestry and coming home to Scotland. These homecomings, whether of individual people, families or larger groups, were individualised, intensely personal, moving experiences, very different to traditional sightseeing-based tourism. Responding to this, VisitScotland embarked on the Ancestral-Scotland initiative, the focus of which is to encourage people to come to Scotland and, sometimes quite literally, walk in the footsteps of their ancestors. The first version of the Ancestral Scotland website was launched in early 2002. The site, which contains ancestral research guidance and access to resources, as well as tourism information, was an immediate success and it has been redeveloped and extended over the years in order to keep pace with the changing needs and expectations of ancestral researchers. Today, it is one of the most visited Scottish tourism-related websites, and it has encouraged and enabled large numbers of people of Scottish ancestry to make their ancestral journey home to touch their past.

AncestralScotland is well represented during Scottish promotions overseas: look out for AncestralScotland activities in North America in particular. It was featured during the 'Scotland at the Smithsonian' events a few years ago, for example, and AncestralScotland is always high profile at Tartan Week in New York.

The aim of the AncestralScotland initiative is to help you touch the past in the ways described in this book. One of the ways that the initiative helps is by ensuring that the service you receive, when you make your ancestral journey to Scotland, is of as high a standard as possible. Staff at tourism businesses, tourist information offices, museums, archives, libraries, and a host of other occupations have the opportunity to attend training events that allow them to learn more about ancestral research and the opportunities for increasing the range and quality of services that are available to you, the ancestral researcher, during your visit. You should look out for businesses or individuals who are members of the Ancestral Tourism Welcome Scheme. These are people who have developed an understanding of ancestral research and who have made a commitment to providing you with the high standards of service needed to ensure that you get the very most from your ancestral journey. They will know where local advice and assistance is available and they may well be actively engaged in ancestral research themselves. If they are, then their advice may be highly useful to you – who knows, you may find that you share an ancestor or two! It has certainly happened before.

Members of the Ancestral Tourism Welcome Scheme will display a logo on their premises. I suppose I am a little biased – I developed the training course – but the scheme really is there to help you. Walking in your ancestors' footsteps is not a cliché: it can make all the research worthwhile and transform your understanding of your ancestral past.

Celebrations

Your connection with Scotland is worth celebrating and you will find plenty of opportunities to join other people in doing so. If you are a member of a clan society or a surname association, you may well find that there are gatherings and homecomings held for you and your fellow members at regular intervals. These events are well worth participating in, not least because you will be in the company of people who share the same interests as you do – perhaps even the same DNA as you – and your hosts will ensure that you get the very best from your visit to Scotland. You will find that most such gatherings share similar objectives – to introduce you to Scotland's culture and its people; to create and extend links between association members; and to have a really good time while doing so. Most gatherings, too, will give you an opportunity to untangle the reality of Scotland and its history from some of the myths and romantic notions that surround it – you will discover that the reality is even more compelling than the myths.

Organised homecomings based on ancestral connections with particular places and regions have been so successful in the past that, given their success, we may look forward to many more in the future. This book began, for example, with the Orkney Homecoming that took place in 1999. This event, with only a relatively small number of participants, had an extremely positive impact, both on participants and the local community. Participants learned about their heritage, their connection with Scotland and, most importantly of all, they learned about themselves. For the community in Orkney there were social and cultural benefits as well as the immediate economic benefits. The local community became stronger and more confident, and more connected, as a result. A second Orkney homecoming is scheduled for May 2007.

2007 is an important year in the Scottish calendar because of Highland 2007: a year-long celebration of Highlands and Islands culture. The aim of Highland 2007 is to celebrate the unique contribution of Highland culture to Scotland in the past, the present and into the future. This legacy is celebrated with six themes – art, sport, heritage, language, environment and science – which will be just as important as the celebration itself. People of Scottish ancestry from around the world are being encouraged to make their ancestral journey back home to Scotland and participate in the celebrations. Visit the Highland 2007 website at www.high-land2007.com for information about the celebration and its extensive calendar of events.

Perhaps the most significant single event in 2007, in terms of Scotland's history, is the opening of the new visitor centre at Culloden and the sensitive, thought-provoking reinterpretation of the historic battlefield. If you have been to Culloden already you know that it is an emotive place to visit; in 2007 the experience will be even more moving. The battlefield will be restored to its original state as on the eve of the battle, which was the last pitched battle to be fought on British soil and at which Bonnie Prince Charlie and his followers were defeated, an event that cemented the future direction of Scotland's history and shattered the young Prince's dreams. Many Highlanders emigrated across the Atlantic after the failure of this rebellion, including Flora MacDonald, from Flodigarry, Skye, who played such a celebrated part in the Prince's ultimately tragic story.

The year 2009 will also be a time of major celebration. It marks the 250th anniversary of the birth of Robert Burns, Scotland's national poet, and perhaps Scotland's best known cultural icon, whose words have appeared in poem and song around the world. The Scottish Executive is promoting 2009 as a year of homecomings, aiming to encourage Scotland's diaspora to come home and join a celebration of our shared heritage. At the time of writing, details of the year's events are not finalised, but they will be publicised widely as soon as they are.

While every ancestral journey to Scotland is a celebration of sorts, remember that there are opportunities, too, to be part of something bigger. As you may well know, Scots love to celebrate.

Exploring the Bigger Picture

You can spend hours on the Internet collecting ancestral research information, days in archives or weeks piecing together a comprehensive family tree, but you will not truly understand your past unless you make an ancestral journey back home to Scotland. You need to touch the past, and the past is here.

Not that an ancestral journey should only involve ancestral research focused on your own forebears. You need to balance a range of activities in order to get the very best from your journey, and you may want to place your own ancestry into the wider context of Scottish history. We sometimes forget that the history we read about in textbooks is about the lives and actions of real people in the past. Your ancestors were some of those people, so perhaps in small ways, unacknowledged at the time, they made Scotland's history. History is not just about the deeds of kings and queens, princes and generals, it is about ordinary people and their daily lives. You should remind yourself of this as you proceed with your ancestral journey.

In deciding how you will explore the bigger picture, you may wish to treat it like unravelling a story. The choice of story is up to you, but having a narrative in mind can transform your ancestral journey. In part the story is of your ancestors, of course – they are your heroes and heroines – but think about the wider story and use that to guide the way you plan your journey. Let me give you an example from my own experience.

A couple of years ago, I visited Culloden battlefield – actually, that isn't true: I only met a colleague for coffee in the restaurant at the visitor centre and took a little time to look very quickly at the exhibition. I knew the general outline of the Jacobite rebellion and the events that brought Bonnie Prince Charlie to this place; I found my visit interesting and yes, quite moving. After all, being at the location of the last pitched battle on British soil and one which determined the fate of your country must affect you in some way. Family tradition has it that one of my ancestors fought at Culloden as a member of the Cameron clan, so the visit touched my own family story. But the visit as a whole was, in a way, frustratingly limited – I actually felt rather guilty for not being more satisfied with the experience of what is, after all, an iconic Scottish site. Thinking about it afterwards, I realised that what I wanted to know more about was the wider story, and I wanted to be able to touch more of my past. In other words, I wanted a narrative, a wider context in which to place my own ancestors and the events of 16 April 1746 at Culloden Moor.

I did some research, and a narrative began to take shape. What also became apparent were a number of places I wanted to visit, real places that were part of the narrative I wanted to explore. It is a fascinating process, developing this sort of plan: it gives real purpose to the journey you undertake as a result. As well as general history books and a short biography of Prince Charles Edward Stuart, I also used a marvellous document available online in the National Library of Scotland's 'Scottish History in Print' collection: Walter Blaikie's *Itinerary of Prince Charles Edward Stuart from his landing in Scotland July 1745 to his departure in September 1746*, first published in 1897. It is available to view at www.nls. uk/print/transcriptions/itinerary.

From this research came my own itinerary for an ancestral journey. Highlights of it included a visit to the Highland Folk Museum's wonderful open air museum in Newtonmore, where an early 1700s Highland township has been reconstructed based on archaeological evidence. *Baile Gean*, or the Township of Goodwill as it is known, is a fascinating insight into life at the time. This prompted me to look at www.ambaile.org, which provides a first class introduction to Highland history and culture. (The site is bilingual, English and Gaelic.) Other highlights I decided to visit were Ruthven Barracks, a lonely and imposing garrison building, now ruinous; Culloden, of course, and Fort George. Fort George, near Inverness, was built in the years after Culloden as both a symbol and a manifest reality of official government power. Make sure you visit Baile Gean first, and then compare the two – there was precious little about goodwill in the purpose and design of Fort George.

Planning an itinerary in this way, on a basis of research into related historical happenings, meant that I learned much more about the background to Culloden and its aftermath, and my resulting visit to the battlefield was a more powerful experience. This is why exploring the bigger picture at the same time as you are undertaking ancestral research is such a good idea.

In case you find it a useful starting point for constructing and exploring your own ancestral narrative, I've included a 1745 Rebellion touring itinerary as an Appendix at the end of the book. Feel free to use it in its entirety, or as a basis for constructing your own. Either way, it will help you touch the past and know it personally.

You can use this itinerary approach for any period in history and for any area. If your ancestors came from one of Scotland's cities and their surrounding regions – Edinburgh, Glasgow, Aberdeen, Dundee, Stirling or Inverness – then use the city as the base for your exploration. Each has its own unique character and set of attractions, and each has a strong, unique identity. Perhaps the character of the people you meet as you construct your own ancestral narrative will help you understand your own make-up better. This is often the case.

One final but important point about this approach to exploring the bigger picture: don't forget that Scotland is much more than archives, museums and historical sites. It is a vibrant, living country as well, so remember to leave space in your journey to explore the other things our country has to offer, such as sports, theatre, music and the outdoors. You and your family or travelling companions should be creating new memories as well as discovering your ancestral homeland.

The future of the past

Opportunities to touch the past in the ways I've described here, and in other ways, look set to increase over the coming years. The past has a bright future, indeed. In Scotland, the Scottish Family History Service Project, described in Chapter 3, will continue the convergence of the family history-related services of the National Archives of Scotland, the General Register Office for Scotland and the Court of the Lord Lyon. Researchers will find increasing amounts of related information becoming available from a single source.

Across Scotland, plans are being discussed for new family history centres. Of course, these all depend on funding being available to pay for the construction or refurbishment of suitable buildings, but it is a mark of just how seriously public agencies are taking the continued interest in ancestral research. Museums, archives and libraries in some areas are looking at ways to work more closely together so that resources and services can be provided to researchers more efficiently in a more coherent, integrated way.

One very exciting potential development is an online emigration museum, drawing together resources from a number of different agencies. 'Museum' is probably the wrong word to describe what is proposed, as it has rather specific connotations, while this project will combine aspects of museums, archives, libraries, study centres and much, much more. The aim will be to provide access to resources that are in Scotland itself but also those of other institutions around the world, so that the global community of people of Scottish ancestry can share resources relevant to the emigration of so many of Scotland's sons and daughters. Discussions about this development are at an early stage and it will be a huge undertaking, but the benefits to researchers, students and anyone wanting to understand Scotland and its emigration heritage are considerable: I really hope that the project goes ahead. Alongside other initiatives, it will encourage even more people to make the journey home to Scotland to touch their past.

Homecoming experiences

With 21st century airline travel, we can accomplish journeys in a day that our ancestors might have spent six or more weeks enduring by boat in the 19th century or earlier. Modern airports, too, have ensured that journey's end generally happens without ceremony or time for reflection. The homecoming journey starts much earlier than the moment you step onto a plane, of course. It begins with the realisation that there is a home to which to travel and that it was once inhabited by people with whom you have a personal, direct and meaningful connection. Making that connection can be an emotional experience. A few years ago, for example, I was at the Scottish Village that had been set up in New York City's Grand Central Station as part of Tartan Week celebrations. I was there to talk to people who wanted advice about ancestral research and ancestral tourism and, courtesy of the General Register Office for Scotland, I had access to the www.scotlandspeople.gov.uk databases via my laptop computer. At lunchtime one day, a very smartly dressed, well groomed and businesslike young woman came up to me and asked for information about her Scottish grandmother. Now, her grandmother's records were too recent, so they were not accessible online. When I told the young lady this, she made to stand up, saying 'Well this is a waste of my time'. I asked her to stay, which she did reluctantly, while I tried to find her great-grandparent's marriage certificate. Up it popped in the index, so I clicked on the 'view image' button and there it was. My businesslike young lady looked at the screen, looked at me, looked back at the screen and began to cry with the shock of finding a real, immediate connection to the past. I do hope she carried on in her journey and did some research of her own.

Many homecomers describe their ancestral journey as something akin to a pilgrimage, or a search for answers about themselves – a sort of spiritual journey. These feelings are deep ones, genuinely felt, and are worthy of respect and sensitivity. When in Scotland it is often important for people to find an actual place that they can touch – the land and stones of a croft, for instance, a house or even a street. It can be upsetting for ancestral researchers if the place that their ancestors knew and called home no longer exists, especially after making such a long journey to see it. Many crofts were abandoned and, with the roofs gone – often taken off by the inhabitants when they left – the buildings soon tumbled down or the stones were reused to build field walls or other structures. Houses could be demolished to make way for new buildings; whole areas of cities such as Glasgow were transformed as tenement housing was torn down and replaced. Sometimes, sadly, not all of the past can be touched today. Where it remains, though, the experience can be a profound one. As one old gentleman said when he saw all that remained of his ancestor's home, a lonely pile of stones on a hillside, 'This is where it all began…'. That feeling of being at home, of being in a special place, is very common and cannot simply be dismissed as peoples' imaginations at work.

Every individual's experience of homecoming is different. For some, it is something personal – intimate, almost – that they may not want to share with others, even in their own family. Indeed, it is partly for this reason that so-called ancestral tourists didn't appear in official statistics until recently. People on a homecoming journey very often don't want to be regarded as 'just' tourists. To them, their journey has a meaning and a purpose that has nothing to do with traditional tourism.

For other people, though, joining with others to celebrate their sense of connection is important, hence the popularity of clan gatherings and the increasing occurrence of organised homecomings. In both of these cases, the opportunity to participate with other like-minded people in organised events is usually what attracts participants. Contact with local people is also very important. We saw this with the 1999 Orkney Homecoming, during which there was a special Gala evening in which local inhabitants and home-comers participated. They were entertained together, ate together and danced together, making it a memorable evening. One of the things that bound the entire group together on the night was the sharing of a Bride's Cog, an Orcadian wedding tradition. The Cog contains a drink made to a (usually) secret recipe and everyone present is encouraged to drink from the communal cog to show their solidarity in celebration. The homecomers quickly discovered not to drink too much, too quickly!

Whether you want to experience your ancestral homecoming in the company of others or prefer to do so alone or with loved ones, whatever the reason and however you do it, my advice is to make, and record, your own ancestral journey – it is one you will never forget.

The morning after the homecoming the night before

I hope that, when you embarked on your homecoming journey, you had some specific aims in mind. You might have wanted to do some local research, or to meet some living relatives. You might have wanted to take photographs of places your ancestors lived or of their gravestones. Or you may simply have wanted to touch the past in one of the other ways that we've discussed. It is worth reflecting on your homecoming experience once you have returned from it, and writing down what you did and how you felt during each step of the journey. In this digital age it might be considered old-fashioned to suggest it, but why not make a scrapbook. Remember that, in most cases, your family tree doesn't stop with you and there will be future generations who will be interested in what you have learned. In having children and grandchildren each of us becomes, in time, part of someone else's past and we have a responsibility to make sure that future ancestral researchers can learn as much about us as possible, as accurately as we can make it. Since we have learned a lot about our past, we should record it in ways that both entertain and inform, and avoid our descendants having to redo all of our research.

In reflecting on your homecoming experience, here are some questions you might like to consider, to which you should write down the answers, perhaps in your homecoming scrapbook. What are the main things you have learned, both in terms of the factual content of your family tree but also about the world in which your ancestors lived? What have you learned, too, about yourself? What new research avenues have you opened up? Are there new branches of the family or long lost relatives you have uncovered perhaps, or are there family stories that need to be researched further? Have you discovered any myths or inaccuracies in the information you already had?

Who did you meet during your homecoming journey? Some of the people may have helped you with advice or in some other way. Even if they were just doing their job it does no harm, and usually a lot of good, to send a note of thanks. Perhaps you met some living relatives with whom you want to keep in touch. Make sure you do this, whether by email, letter or even just a card at Christmas time – keeping the connections going is just as important as making them in the first place.

Finally, will you repeat the ancestral journey or even undertake a new one? Many people find that, having 'returned' to Scotland, they want to do so again. It may be because they didn't plan their research properly and ran out of time – one way of avoiding this is by making appointments to visit archives and family history society offices at the beginning of your trip rather than at the end, which allows time to revisit the resources if you need to do so before you leave. Not being able to do so because you did not visit until the end of your journey can lead to disappointment. Or you may want to visit Scotland again simply because of the strength of the connection you feel, the relatives you have discovered and the friends you have made. I know one Canadian couple who liked to return so often they decided to buy a house in the Highlands, and they are trying to persuade their daughter to study at a Scottish university. The important thing to remember is that a homecoming is not the journey's end; there is no final destination. There will always be more to discover about your connections to your past.

The main message of this chapter has been that you need to touch the past in order to be able to understand it, and that in order to touch it you must make an ancestral journey back home to Scotland. More and more people are doing so, and to make sure that homecomers get the very best from their experience, individuals, businesses, organisations and indeed the Scottish Executive itself is working to provide the best possible services and the easiest access to ancestral research resources for visitors. This brings benefits not only to you, but also to Scotland's current population, contributing to its economic and social wellbeing and to its cultural richness as well. In the next chapter we will consider some aspects of Scotland's lively, dynamic, distinctive and internationally well-known culture and heritage, for they too may be part of why you feel rooted in Scotland.

CHAPTER 6

Roots Revealed: Cultural Connection

WHAT IS 'SCOTTISH'? Why does it matter, and how is Scottish culture manifested? Exploring and understanding Scotland's culture can deepen and enrich your sense of connection with Scotland and its people, and doing so is as much part of your ancestral journey as tracing the births, marriages and deaths of your ancestors. This chapter of *Rooted in Scotland* explores a variety of aspects of Scotland's culture. Earlier, I said that in order to understand Scotland's past you need to touch it – now, I say that in order to understand Scotland's culture you need to be part of it. Participate, even if only as a member of the audience.

The majority of Scots will say that they are Scottish first and British second. Most are comfortable with that dual sense of identity and don't see pride in being Scottish as in some way anti-British or anti-English. This sense of Scottishness is expressed in a number of ways, and we will look at some of them here. Inevitably, this is a personal selection and there may well be things with which you disagree, or things you expected to see but which are not included – in a way, I hope that this is so. If there is one thing that all Scots like, it is a good debate, an airing of issues and a sharing of opinions.

Government, in our case in the form of the Scottish Executive, has taken a keen interest in Scotland's cultural life since the Scottish Parliament came into being in 1999. Culture, after all, is arguably what makes us human and certainly our cultural values underpin our sense of national consciousness. I don't intend, here, to get into a debate about nationalism or the question of whether or not Scotland should be an independent country: you can make your own mind up about that. When I refer to national consciousness I am referring simply to that sense of shared identity and common values that unites people from the same country.

Our Scottish Executive's commitment to culture was expressed through the establishment of a Cultural Commission, charged with carrying out a review of Scotland's culture and with making recommendations towards promoting and developing it. Having received the Commission's report, the Scottish Executive published its culture policy statement in a 2006 document called *Scotland's Culture*. It is available for download from the Executive's website at www.scotland.gov.uk.

Devolution

Prior to the Act of Union, which combined the English and Scottish Parliaments in 1707, Scotland had its own sovereign Parliament, even though the crowns had been united under a single monarch since 1603. From 1707 onwards a single Parliament, based in London, legislated for the whole of the United Kingdom. The Act of Union was not simply the extension of the English system of government to Scotland, however; the Act enshrined some of the significant differences between the two countries. For example, Scotland retains its own judiciary system, Scots law, which is a separate (and arguably better, though I admit as a Scot that I am biased) system to that which applies elsewhere in Great Britain. Scotland also has a separate education system, one that is widely admired for the quality of the education that Scotland's young people receive. Finally, another area of difference is in Scotland's banking system. There are three Scottish banks which each issue their own banknotes and these are all accepted in Scotland, alongside Bank of England notes, as payment. (Apparently, under Scots law, none of these four banknotes are legal tender, because Scots law lacks this concept!)

Despite having a number of differences written into the terms of the Act of Union, and in spite of the number of Scottish politicians who have been able to make careers for themselves in the UK Parliament, the end of the 20th century saw an increasing desire for the distinctive character of Scotland to be recognised by constitutional change. A referendum was held in Scotland in 1997, asking voters whether they wanted a Scottish Parliament. The majority were in favour of a Parliament with tax varying powers and accordingly, in 1998, The Scotland Act was passed, which devolved a range of powers to a new Scottish Parliament.

This concept of devolution is an interesting one and is worth explaining in greater detail. The UK Parliament can, if it wishes, still legislate on devolved matters in Scotland – in other words, it remains sovereign. By convention, however, it does not do so without the agreement of the Scottish Parliament, and legislation specific to Scotland, concerning a wide range of topics, is debated and enacted by the Scottish Parliament alone. Certain matters such as defence, immigration, and foreign relations are, in any case reserved by the UK Parliament. Elected politicians known as MSPs (Members of the Scottish Parliament) make up the Scottish Parliament, which meets in a striking (and not uncontroversial) building at Holyrood in central Edinburgh. The devolved government of Scotland is called the Scottish Executive, and is headed by a First Minister who is assisted by a number of Ministerial colleagues. This devolved system of government has quickly become part of Scotland's wider identity. If you wish to know more about the Scottish Parliament and the Scottish Executive and its work, you will find details at their websites, www.scottish.parliament.uk and www.scotland.gov.uk, respectively.

The Performing Arts

The performing arts are a fundamentally important part of Scotland's cultural mix and a rich source of creativity and vitality of expression. Let's start with music. Perhaps the most iconic Scottish music is that played on the bagpipes, either by a single piper or played en masse by a pipe band. Bagpipes are known from other parts of the world, of course; they are an ancient instrument and are not unique to Scotland. In Scotland, however, they have become associated with the wearing of tartan and the whole image of 'traditional' dress and music. Whatever your views on 'tartanry' and some of the myths of Scottish heritage, surely there are few people who will fail to be stirred by the music of a good piper.

Scottish music traditions encompass sung folk music too, whether performed in Gaelic or English. Gaelic is a beautiful, poetic language with a rich history: even the most mundane of stories, poetry or song sound haunting and romantic when rendered in Gaelic. Fiddle playing is also an important part of the folk tradition, with unique regional variations in playing style from Shetland to the Borders. One of the most astonishing musical events I've ever experienced was a performance by massed fiddlers: the music swelled and grew and filled the hall with extraordinary sound and energy. There is also a vibrant classical music scene, and the work of the national companies in opera, chamber music and orchestral music is internationally recognised. Even though its musical traditions are steeped in heritage, don't think that Scottish music is backward-looking. There is a huge variety of contemporary folk, jazz, and rock acts – a lively, dynamic music scene.

In dance, too, Scottish performers are rooted in their traditions but are also committed to the creation of new forms of expression. Traditional dance such as Scottish country dancing is increasingly a favourite with locals and visitors alike, and can often be experienced at a *céilidh* (pron. *kay-lee*) – a heady mixture of music, song and dance. There is also an important Highland dance tradition, with competitions held every year at community Highland games, and of course Scottish Ballet is Scotland's national dance company.

Scottish theatre has perhaps not been as well known as some of the other performing arts, but the Scottish Executive's decision in 2003 to create a National Theatre of Scotland has changed the theatre landscape tremendously. The National Theatre does not have a permanent building; instead it concentrates on taking its performances to audiences across Scotland and beyond. It is an exciting, innovative project, about which you can learn more at www.nationaltheatrescotland.com.

Before we move on to examine the visual arts, a word about the screen. Scotland has a long tradition in the screen industries and there are many fine Scottish films. Despite its commercial success, I am not thinking of *Braveheart* here, but smaller films such as my two favourites, *Local Hero* and *Whisky Galore* (or *Tight Little Island*, as it was renamed for its North American release). Both *Local Hero* and *Whisky Galore* capture something of the sense of community, and of fun, that is typically Scottish. A few years ago I showed *Whisky Galore* at an event in New York and although the audience was not attuned to the dialect and could understand only perhaps one word in ten, we had an uproarious evening because the visual humour of the film was so engaging. The Edinburgh International Film Festival takes place every August, and today's aspiring film makers have a tremendous opportunity thanks to the recently launched Scottish Screen Academy, also based in Edinburgh. Have a look at www.screenacademyscotland.co.uk if you are interested in finding out more.

The Visual Arts

The diversity, creativity and fusion of the traditional and the contemporary evident in the performing arts also have parallels in the visual arts. Scotland has a depth of artistic tradition arguably extending back to the Stone Age, but certainly evident in the striking designs on Pictish carved stones. The nation has a wealth of galleries – whether the larger galleries of Edinburgh and Glasgow or the many smaller, more intimate galleries scattered across the country.

Painting, sculpture, photography and craftwork are evident wherever your ancestral journey takes you, and an appreciation of the visual arts can help you get a deeper understanding of this aspect of your heritage. For example, weaving was a key industry across southern central Scotland, from Dundee to the outskirts of

Glasgow, so if your family stems from there you may be part of a great textile tradition.

Many of Scotland's more recent artists have international reputations – two favourites of mine are the sculptor Sir Eduardo Paolozzi and the architect, designer and painter Charles Rennie Mackintosh. Paolozzi was born in Leith in 1924, the son of Italian immigrants. He was a founder of the Independent Group, which presaged the Pop Art movement of the 1960s, and produced a large and influential body of work, much of which was gifted to the Scottish National Gallery of Modern Art. You can find out more about this and Scotland's other national galleries at www.nationalgalleries.org.

Mackintosh was born in Glasgow in 1868 and is famous as a designer in the Arts and Crafts movement, and as a leader in Art Nouveau in Scotland. He was responsible for a number of strikingly attractive buildings, many of them in Glasgow. His Glasgow School of Art building is often described as one of the finest buildings in Britain. You can learn more about his life and works at www.crmsociety.com, the website of the Charles Rennie Mackintosh Society.

Finally in this brief account of some of Scotland visual arts, many people searching for an expression of Scotland's culture will look for the output of Scotland's craftsmen and women. Craftwork is often seen as more accessible than some other forms of artistic expression and offers the benefit of being able to purchase pieces for your own use or pleasure. From jewellery to pottery and from tapestry to glasswork, there are craftspeople at work throughout Scotland every day. You may visit many of these artists as they work, for example the pottery painters at Highland Stoneware in Lochinver and Ullapool. Many of these artists draw inspiration from their own feelings of rootedness and connection with Scotland's heritage and landscapes, and you can see this expressed in their work. Look, for example, at the work of tapestry artist Leila Thomson at www.hoxatapestrygallery.co.uk. For a searchable directory of Scotland's craftspeople, visit www. craftscotland.org.

Tartan

Many would argue that tartan is a visual art, of a sort. Tartan, whether in the form of the kilt or in one of its myriad other decorative forms, is an iconic symbol of Scottishness. The word 'tartan' is probably derived from the French *terataine*, a kind of cloth. The early plaid, or tartan, was a large piece of woven material that was wrapped around the body. In winter it could take the place of a cloak; if allowed to become wet, the material trapped a warm layer of air between it and the wearer, enabling him to stay warm and snug during a night spent on a Scottish hillside. This large cloth – known as a *feile breacan,* was in time separated into an upper and lower part, the lower of which was known as a *feile beag,* Anglicised to philabeg or kilt.

The design of a tartan is known as its sett. Prior to 1745, so-called 'district' tartans had begun to emerge simply because weavers in different areas of the country had different styles, colour dyes or threads available to them, but there was no 'clan tartan' as such. For those who could afford it, the choice of tartan was doubtless more a fashion statement based on colour and weave style than a symbol of affiliation to a particular clan. And there is no ancient historical foundation for the symbolism now attached to the colours used in the sett.

During the 1745 rebellion, tartans were not yet used as uniforms: the opposing sides wore coloured cockades on their hats to differentiate friend from foe. Despite a persisting myth, Charles Edward Stuart – Bonnie Prince Charlie – did not arrive in Scotland kilted and ready for battle. Upon his arrival, he was described by a contemporary eyewitness as 'a tall youth of a most agreeable aspect, in a plain black coat with a plain shirt not very clean'[32]. Smartly attired – apart from the shirt – but hardly heroic.

---

[32] Page 41 of Fitzroy Maclean *Bonnie Prince Charlie,* 1989, Canongate Publishing, Edinburgh, quoting a contemporary account of a meeting with the Prince.

As we know, however, the rebellion was unsuccessful, leading to the end of the clan system as the basis of Highland life, to harsh government repression and to the destruction of Prince Charlie's dreams on the battlefield of Culloden. In 1746 tartan was proscribed – meaning that wearing it was forbidden to everyone but those soldiers in the government's service. In fact, the government became so paranoid that a court of law declared the bagpipe to be a military weapon (a weapon of mass motivation and morale I suppose) and punished a piper, James Reid, as a rebel accordingly.

By 1782, memories of the rebellion had faded, the potential of Highland dress as a military uniform was becoming clear and the official proscription of a style of clothing was seen as unnecessary. Wearing tartan became legal again, and persisted especially in the Highland regiments whose soldiers were valued so highly. In 1822, Highland dress became ultra fashionable due to King George IV's visit to Scotland, which was carefully choreographed and stage managed by that master of the romantic, Sir Walter Scott. The wheel had turned full circle and Edinburgh society – so terrified and appalled by the 'barbarian' Highlanders in 1745 – now embraced tartan and the kilt with gusto. Wearing tartan became not just socially acceptable but indeed a fashion necessity.

Some so-called 'traditions' related to tartan, such as 'clan tartans' were invented by Lowland businessmen, intent on capitalising on the tartan boom. Queen Victoria's love of Scotland and all things associated with it reinforced these practices and laid the foundations for today's perception of tartan and its use in all things decorative. Over 250 years ago, frantic citizens of Edinburgh had boarded up their shops as the Highlanders advanced towards the city: today, Edinburgh has an array of some of the finest kilt shops in Scotland.

Nowadays, tartan is a visible and much celebrated manifestation of clan heritage. Tartans are even recorded by the Court of the Lord Lyon to ensure the individuality of each sett or pattern. Purists may argue at length about the finer points of tartan etiquette and the precise details of how and when to wear it, but most people are content to wear the tartan of their choice as a symbol of their connection with Scotland and in celebration of their heritage.

Events and Festivals

We looked at events and festivals earlier in *Rooted in Scotland* where, in particular, I drew attention to the Highland 2007 celebrations and the 2009 Year of Homecoming. I suggested, also, that you look out for local events in the area of Scotland with which you have an ancestral connection, perhaps timing your own ancestral journey accordingly. Here, I'd like to discuss two additional things: Edinburgh's festivals, and the Highland Games and Gatherings that take place worldwide.

The Edinburgh Festival held in August each year is world famous. It is, however, actually six separate festivals which overlap with one another. There is the Edinburgh International Festival, the Edinburgh Festival Fringe (said to be in its own right the world's largest arts event, with over one million performance tickets sold each year), the Edinburgh International Film Festival, the Edinburgh International Book Festival, the Edinburgh Jazz and Blues Festival and the Edinburgh Television Festival. Although it is not a festival *per se* there is also the Edinburgh Military Tattoo. If you want to experience a quite exceptional concentration and variety of cultural experiences all in a single small city, then Edinburgh is the place to be in August.

Closer to more traditional, as opposed to contemporary, culture are the many Highland Games and Gatherings held worldwide. They range from modest local events to crowd-drawing phenomena such as the Grandfather Mountain games in North Carolina, which attracts about 30,000 people each year. Some people criticise such events, saying that they celebrate a vision of Scotland that is clouded by myth, is backward-looking and focused on a Highland heritage that isn't representative of Scotland as a whole, perhaps not even of the Highlands themselves. Perhaps; they may have a point in that we ought to celebrate Scotland as it is, not as how we dream it may have been, but the fact remains that Highland Games and Gatherings have grown from authentic roots. As celebrations of a shared sense of connection – of being rooted in Scotland – they are to be applauded, encouraged and most of all, attended. There are several useful websites with international listings of games and events. Try **www.usscots.com** for these, which is sponsored by The Scots Heritage Society.

Clans and Family Associations

It is worth returning to events and festivals, clan and family associations to discuss them in the wider context of Scottish culture. Many would say that the clan as a concept and clans in reality as associations have a renewed importance today. Clans, tribes and family groups comprise a global network of people with a shared heritage transcending national boundaries. They bring people together in celebration of their heritage and with a shared desire to travel together – or at least in the same general direction – on their ancestral journeys.

The quality of clan associations depends to large extent on the Chief and the others who manage clan activities. If the Chief is not interested in fostering the clan association it may struggle, but many Chiefs or heads of tribes or families see the merit in encouraging the development of bonds between Clan members, not for profit but for wider benefits. A search for your surname on Google or any other Internet search engine will find details of your clan association if one exists. I recommend that you consider joining and participating actively in making the association stronger, but do keep things in perspective. Society has changed a lot since the days of the clans, and whatever clans may have been in the past, the relationship between clan members and chief and clan today is very different.

Language Traditions

In modern Scotland, English is the most commonly spoken language. This general statement hides a lot of history however, because there are several linguistic traditions in evidence, foremost among which are Scottish Gaelic, Scots and Norse.

In the Highlands, particularly in the west and north, Gaelic was the dominant language for centuries (though in mediaeval times it was spoken as far south as Edinburgh). You can still hear it spoken today in these areas. I visited a school on the island of Islay recently, at which a children's nursery was run entirely in Gaelic. I don't speak a word of the language, so felt hopelessly inadequate in the face of the happily chattering youngsters who will grow up completely bilingual. Intensive efforts to keep the language alive in speech and writing appear to be succeeding and you will, for instance, find place names in both English and Gaelic on many signposts as you drive around. (It should be noted that, while very closely related, Irish Gaelic and Scottish are distinctly different languages.)

If your ancestors were from this Gaelic-speaking region and you would like to learn this ancient yet living language, an ideal starting point is *Sabhal Mòr Ostaig*, Scotland's only Gaelic college, at www.smo.uhi.ac.uk. The college offers a range of courses, including those for complete beginners. If you are interested in exploring the richness and contemporary creativity of Gaelic Arts more generally, the best starting point is the website of the Gaelic Arts agency, *Proiseact nan Ealan*, at www.gaelic-arts.com.

For most of the rest of Scotland, Scots is the predominant dialect. People argue about whether Scots is a language or a dialect, but both Gaelic and Scots were recognised under the European Charter for Regional or Minority Languages, giving it true language status. It has regional variations, of course: in northeast Scotland, the area around Aberdeen, the dialect is called Doric. In Ulster, it is Ulster Scots. Elsewhere it is Lallans, or Lowland Scots.

In Orkney and Shetland, too, you will hear distinctive dialects, at times more Scandinavian than English or Scots. In fact, some Scandinavian visitors find themselves surprised when they hear familiar sounding words used in these areas. Orkney and Shetland were once part of the Viking world – indeed, they were pledged by the King of Denmark in 1468 as a dowry for his daughter to marry to King James III – and many of the dialect words still used in these islands today have their origins in Old Norse.

If you spend enough time in Scotland you'll begin to notice regional differences in spoken accents, and it can be fun trying to 'place' people. If you have an ancestral connection with a particular place you should bear in mind that, because spoken accents and dialect words can be very long-lasting, the language or dialect that you hear may be the same as that which your ancestors spoke.

Literature and Storytelling

The written word is as important to Scots as the spoken word – in fact, some would probably argue that it is more important. It is a fact that Scotland has a long and distinguished literary tradition. It may be that the nation's long-standing commitment to education fuelled this, creating a demand for literature and a population with questioning minds prepared to debate, challenge and contribute.

Robert Burns is probably Scotland's best known author (though it is debatable whether the hundreds of thousands of people who sing *Auld Lang Syne* at Hogmanay – the Scots term for New Year's Eve – actually know who is responsible for writing it). Burns' life and work is celebrated worldwide, each January 25, at Burns Suppers: celebrations in poetry, song and fellowship that commemorate the day of the Bard's birth. For a comprehensive introduction to the man and his work, visit www.robertburns.org. A special celebration is planned to mark the 250th anniversary of Burns' birth in 2009.

We met another of Scotland's well known authors, Robert Louis Stevenson, in Chapter 2. Stevenson, born in Edinburgh in 1850, was the son and grandson of the so-called 'Lighthouse Stevensons', a family of distinguished lighthouse designers and engineers. He travelled widely and wrote prolifically, including such classics as *Treasure Island*, *The Strange Case of Dr Jekyll and Mr Hyde*, and the Scotland-based *Kidnapped* and its sequel *Catriona*.

The list of writers could go on and on, right through to well known modern writers such as Ian Rankin, Iain Banks and Alexander McCall Smith, to name just three personal favourites. Good literature is a fusion of experience and imagination, so one could say that all Scottish writers are, at least in part, firmly rooted in Scotland. One route to an understanding of Scotland, therefore, is via its literature.

Another route to cultural understanding, equally important, is through oral storytelling traditions, more ancient than their written cousin. A centuries-old tradition of oral storytelling has enabled us to pass down stories that are hundreds of years old from generation to generation. Today, visit any good pub on any given day and you will hear stories still being told in the form of anecdotes, reminiscences, jokes and the sharing of (sometimes diverging) opinion. More formal storytelling traditions also exist, and the Scottish Storytelling Centre (www.scottishstorytellingcentre.co.uk) is a good place to learn more. There are often local storytelling events, so look out for them when you make your ancestral journey home to Scotland. I have a friend who runs an excellent seafood restaurant in Scrabster, in the north of Scotland; in order to add some variety to his guests' experience, he hosts periodic storytelling evenings at which a storyteller punctuates dinner with entertaining, absorbing traditional stories. These evenings have proven enormously popular with local people and visitors to the area, and the tradition of storytelling in Scotland continues to thrive due to the presence of events like these.

Sport

Sport is sometimes overlooked as an aspect of cultural identity but it surely deserves an honourable mention. Scotland is, after all, the 'home of golf' and the game is certainly a popular pastime. Golf is popular with visiting ancestral researchers or, more often, their spouses, who may share some of their partners' interest but not their enthusiasm for archives.

Scotland's national sporting associations – such as the Football Association and the Scottish Rugby Union – ensure that the country has independent representation in some major sporting events. Scottish athletes can compete for their country in the Commonwealth Games, but for the Olympic Games they must gain a place in the British team – an interesting manifestation of the Scottish-British duality.

Scotland's football leagues are competitive, particular the Premier League in which, among others, the internationally known Celtic, Rangers and Hearts play. Years ago, Scottish football supporters did not have a terribly good international reputation but nowadays the 'Tartan Army' that follows the national football team – more in enthusiasm than expectation – is renowned worldwide as an example of how fans can be passionate supporters of their team and ambassadors for their country simultaneously.

In rugby too, Scotland is well served by its ambassadors, both the players and the passionate yet well-behaved supporters. My erstwhile next-door neighbour still comes to visit in order to watch televised rugby matches whenever Scotland's national team plays. A grown man, his wife objects to him kneeling in front of the television, shouting and pleading or holding his head in his hands with despair when things don't go quite as well as they ought, though he is merely reflecting what is happening elsewhere at Murrayfield stadium.

Curling and shinty – a traditional game similar to hurling in Ireland – are also popular, though they lack the same mass appeal as golf, football and rugby. The number of people involved in curling, however, is on the rise due to the spectacular success of the UK Women's curling team – all of whom were Scottish – which won the gold medal at the 2002 Winter Olympics. The Scottish Executive strongly supports sporting activities, both as an expression of Scotland's national identity and for the more mundane but equally important reason that we do not, as individuals, get nearly enough exercise.

Politics

As an illustration of how Scots are at the very heart of Britain, you need to look no further than British politics. As I write this book, Tony Blair is Prime Minister, and the debate about whether the Chancellor, Gordon Brown, should succeed him is rumbling away. The leaders of the Liberal Democratic and Conservative Parties, Menzies Campbell and David Cameron respectively, look on from the sidelines. At the Labour Party conference, ex-President Bill Clinton has just given a rousing, thought-provoking speech. Tony Blair, Gordon Brown and Menzies Campbell were all born in Scotland; David Cameron is of Scottish ancestry; and Bill Clinton is of Ulster-Scots ancestry. Nobody can accuse Scots of letting themselves be excluded from power in politics in Britain, nor for that matter in the US.

Scots have a strong and positive sense of identity, wherever in the world they are. You can experience aspects of Scottish culture wherever you live and this chapter has noted some websites that can help you do this. Two further sites also deserve mention here, both of which were developed by the Scottish Executive in order to reach out to Scots worldwide. The sites are www.scotlandistheplace.com and www.friendsofscotland.gov.uk, each of which provides access to the lively, interesting e-zine *Scotland-Now*. Scotland has a rich, diverse culture, an exploration of which will expand your sense of what it is to be Scottish and will help explain your sense of connection. You need to understand that sense of connection in light of the reality of Scotland's heritage and contemporary life, not through some of the more romanticised notions about Scotland's past. That is not to say that the romantic notions should be dismissed or belittled, just that we need to recognise them for what they are and maintain pride in Scotland's contemporary, distinctive sense of identity. The duality of Scottishness-Britishness need not be a cause of any confusion or lack of confidence. Scots and their culture have had a positive influence throughout Britain and continue to contribute much to its society today.

CHAPTER 7

Roots Reinforced

AS WE NEAR THE END of our journey, it is time to take stock of what we have discovered together thus far. Setting the background, we looked at the meaning of births, marriages and deaths as the punctuation marks in your family's journey from the past and into the future, where we ourselves become ancestors. There are good reasons why you may feel rooted in Scotland and these include feelings of 'home' and a deep personal attachment to your ancestral homeland.

Emigration involved the departure from a homeland and a long, sometimes difficult transition to a new home elsewhere. Sutherland Simpson Taylor's journey has universal relevance, echoing the journeys of so many other emigrants, including author Robert Louis Stevenson, who used his journey as the basis for two books of travel writing.

The popularity of ancestral research means that there is a wealth of resources available to you as you embark on your own ancestral journey. These 'routes to roots' offer a choice of directions for your research and the choice of which route to take is very much a personal one. There is plenty of advice and encouragement to be had along the way, from professionals and from fellow do-it-yourself researchers.

To truly understand your sense of connection with Scotland, however, and to understand your ancestral past, you need to reach out and touch it, and that means a visit (or visits) to Scotland. The AncestralScotland website is there to help you make your ancestral journey back home, and the Highland Year of Culture in 2007 and the Year of Homecoming in 2009 offer the perfect opportunities to arrange your journey to coincide with one of these major celebrations of Scottish culture and heritage. As anyone who has experienced it can confirm, a homecoming journey to Scotland is a special experience whether done as part of a larger event or completed on your own.

Understanding Scottish culture and heritage will, in turn, help you understand your connection with Scotland. Our Scottishness and sense of identity is expressed in many ways, including in our performing and visual arts, in literature, events and festivals, language traditions, politics, clans and the wearing of tartan.

Themes and Variations

Reading *Rooted in Scotland*, you will have become aware of some recurrent themes: the importance of touching the past in order to know it; the benefits to your understanding of becoming part of Scottish culture rather than a passive observer of it; the benefits of making your own ancestral journey back home to Scotland. There is one overarching theme however, and that is the importance of celebrating your Scottish ancestry, knowing who you are, where you came from, and feeling proud of it.

Changing as we Speak

The ways in which you can explore and celebrate your ancestral connection are changing almost as we speak. There are exciting new projects, such as the proposed Highland Archive Centre which received funding as this book was being written. This new archive for the Highlands' past is part of Highland Council's celebration of Highland 2007 and will be opened in 2009, the Scottish Year of Homecoming.

There are rich new resources also becoming available. Again, as this book was being written a new website was launched containing over 40,000 records relating to the people and places of the Outer Hebrides, Scotland's western isles. The www.hebrideanconnections.com website is a wonderful complement to the equally useful www.ambaile.org site with its collection of Gaelic material.

From the Convener

Councillor Stephen Hagan

Council Offices, Kirkwall, Orkney, KW15 1NY

Tel: (01856) 873535   Fax: (01856) 877292   E-mail: convener@orkney.gov.uk

ORKNEY
ISLANDS COUNCIL

Our Ref: SH/AB/JL

23 January 2006

An Open Letter to North Americans of Orcadian Ancestry

Throughout its long history, Orkney's young men and women have sought adventure, challenge and new lives in places far from their homes. For people accustomed to the sea, distances were perhaps not the obstacle we might think, but time has now separated us.

Today's Orcadians are proud of their rich heritage and their ancestral connections with people and communities on the other side of the Atlantic Ocean. As part of Orkney's Diaspora we hope that you share that pride in our common ancestry.

In order to celebrate that connection, and on behalf of the people of Orkney, we would like to invite you to return home to Orkney in May 2007 when there will be special events, tours and access to enthusiastic experts who will help you complete your own personal ancestral journey. There is more information, including how to book, at www.orkneyhomecoming.com

You have been away for a while. It is time to come home.

Yours sincerely

Stephen Hagan
Convener

Alistair Buchan
Chief Executive

'You have been away for a while...' An open letter from
Orkney Islands Council extending an invitation to
North Americans to come home to Orkney in May 2007.
© Seabridge Consultants.

New techniques are being developed and popularised, too. DNA analysis has been applied to ancestral research with great effect and there are some ground-breaking projects being undertaken. Have a look at www.oxfordancestors.com and www.familytreedna.com for examples and more information. There are plenty of other sites and services available and I am sure that DNA-based ancestral research will feature strongly in a future revised and updated edition of *Rooted in Scotland.*

Reflections on the Present

In focusing on our past, and ancestral research as a way of exploring and understanding it, we should not forget that emigration, such a defining moment in many family histories, is still commonplace today.

Scotland, like the rest of Britain, has seen waves of immigrants from a variety of countries, as the innovative website, www.movinghere.org.uk, explains with regard to England. Today we are seeing increasing numbers of European migrants as more countries join the European Union. Understanding the past will help us understand the experience of these modern immigrants. People from Britain continue to migrate, too. A recent BBC report drew attention to increasing numbers of emigrants from the UK, the most popular destinations for whom were Australia, Spain, Canada, New Zealand and the US. In 2004, some 350,000 people left Britain for a new life abroad.

Journey's End

Your sense of connection with Scotland – that feeling of being rooted in Scotland – is something that you should value and celebrate. Exploring it is a journey, but in many ways this ancestral journey has no end – there will always be more to discover and, by sharing your own experiences, more to contribute to the journeys of others. I wish you well with your own journey of discovery.

Appendix 1

Further Reading

THERE IS A WEALTH of good books about Scotland, its history, ancestral research there and related topics. Here is a small selection, most of which are referred to elsewhere in *Rooted in Scotland*. A good way of keeping up to date with new books on Scotland is the excellent bi-monthly magazine *History Scotland*, available at www.historyscotland.com.

Burnett, Charles J & Dennis, Mark D: *Scotland's Heraldic Heritage*, Edinburgh, 1997.

Calder, Jenni: *Scots in Canada*, Edinburgh, 2003.
    Scots in the USA, Edinburgh, 2006.

Cory, Kathleen B: *Tracing Your Scottish Ancestry*, Edinburgh, 2004.

Devine, TM: *The Scottish Nation 1700-2000*, London, 1999.

Harper, Marjory: *Adventurers and Exiles*, London, 2003.

Hunter, James: *Scottish Exodus*, Edinburgh, 2005.

James, Alwyn: *Scottish Roots*, Edinburgh, 2002.

Kennedy, Billy: *Our Most Priceless Heritage*, Belfast, 2005.

Martine, Roddy: *Scottish Clan and Family Names*, Edinburgh, 1992.

National Archives of Scotland: *Tracing Your Scottish Ancestors*, Edinburgh, 2003.

Scottish Executive: *New Strategy for Scottish Tourism*, Edinburgh, 2000.

Pomery, Chris: *DNA and Family History*, Kew, 2004.

Roulston, Dr William J: *Researching Scots-Irish Ancestors*, Belfast, 2005.

Sinclair, Cecil: *Jock Tamson's Bairns*, Edinburgh, 2000.
Tracing Scottish Local History, Edinburgh, 1996.

Appendix II

Useful Websites

THE INTERNET IS A wonderful source of information and a good way to explore your Scottish ancestry from a distance. This book includes a large number of website addresses so that you can find more information and follow up things of particular interest or relevance to your ancestral research from anywhere in the world.

Website addresses often change, however, so this appendix contains only a few main addresses. One of these is www.rootedinscotland.com, which complements the *Rooted in Scotland* book and includes all of the web links mentioned, arranged by chapter. You just need to click on them to visit the sites. These links will be kept up-to-date and relevant new ones will be added as they become available. The *Rooted in Scotland* website also has some additional information that might be useful to your search, and there is an opportunity to leave your comments on the book, as well as your views on what might be included in future editions. I would also be delighted to hear about your own connections with Scotland, and I wish you the best of luck with your ancestral journey.

Three main websites to get you started are below, while a listing of all websites mentioned in this book follows.

www.rootedinscotland.com Complements this book.

www.scotlandspeople.gov.uk Official government records of births, marriages and deaths, and a wealth of other resources.

www.ancestralscotland.com Ancestral tourism website designed to help you get started with ancestral research and get the most from your ancestral journey.

Ancestral Research and Information – General

Am Baile – www.ambaile.org

Ancestral Scotland tourism website – www.ancestralscotland.com

Association of Scottish Genealogists and Researchers in Archives (ASGRA) – www.asgra.co.uk

Callendar House Museum www.falkirk.gov.uk/cultural/museums/museums.htm

Charles Rennie Mackintosh Society – www.crmsociety.com

Contemporary immigration to the UK: *see* Moving Here website

Court of the Lord Lyon King of Arms – www.lyon-court.com

Craftspeople in Scotland Directory – www.craftscotland.org

Culloden Visitor Centre – www.culloden.org.uk

Culloden Battlefield Memorial Project – www.culloden.org

DNA-based ancestral research – www.oxfordancestors.com and www.familytreedna.com

Eden Court Theatre, Inverness – www.eden-court.co.uk

Edinburgh Castle: *see* Historic Scotland

Electric Scotland – www.electricscotland.com

Alastair McIntyre – www.electricscotland.net

Gaelic Arts agency/*Proiseact nan Ealan* – www.gaelic-arts.com

Gaelic history: *see* Am Baile

Genuki – **Gen**ealogy United **K**ingdom and **I**reland – www.genuki.org.uk

The Glasgow Story – www.theglasgowstory.com

Glenfinnan Visitors Centre: *see* National Trust for Scotland

Hebridean Connections – www.hebrideanconnections.com

Highland 2007 – www.highland2007.com

Highland Council – www.highland.gov.uk

Highland Family History Society – www.highlandfhs.org.uk

Highland Folk Museums at Kingussie and Newtownmore – www.highlandfolk.com

History Scotland magazine – www.historyscotland.com

The International Genealogical Index (IGI) – www.familysearch.org

Inverness Museum – www.invernessmuseum.com

Mackay Country – www.mackaycountry.com

The Mitchell Library, Glasgow – www.mitchelllibrary.org or www.glasgow.gov.uk/en/visitors/familyhistory/

Moving Here website – www.movinghere.org.uk

National Library of Scotland – www.nls.uk

Maps at the NLS – www.nls.uk/digitallibrary/map
Walter Blaikie's *Itinerary of Prince Charles Edward Stuart from his landing in Scotland July 1745 to his departure in September 1746*, 1897 – www.nls.uk/print/transcriptions/itinerary

National Theatre of Scotland – www.nationaltheatrescotland.com

The National Trust for Scotland – www.nts.org.uk

Open University – www.open.ac.uk

Origins Network – www.originsnetwork.com

Prestoungrange Gothenburg Visitor Centre – www.prestoungrange.org

Proiseact nan Ealan/Gaelic Arts agency – www.gaelic-arts.com

Robert Burns – www.robertburns.org

Ruthven Barracks, *see* Historic Scotland

Sabhal Mòr Ostaig – www.smo.uhi.ac.uk

The Scotsman archives – http://archive.scotsman.com

Scottish Archive Network (SCAN) – www.scan.org.uk

Scottish Handwriting – www.scottishhandwriting.com

Scottish Association of Family History Societies –
   www.safhs.org.uk

Scottish Family History Service project –
   www.scotlandspeoplehub.gov.uk

Scottish Genealogy Society – www.scotsgenealogy.com

Scottish Museums Council – www.scottishmuseums.org.uk

Scottish National Galleries – www.nationalgalleries.org

Scottish Roots – www.scottishroots.com

Scottish Screen Academy – www.screenacademyscotland.co.uk

Scottish Storytelling Centre – www.scottishstorytellingcentre.co.uk

Scottish Tourist Board, *see* VisitScotland

Society of Genealogists – www.sog.org.uk

Standing Council of Scottish Chiefs – www.myclan.com

Stevenson, Robert Louis. *The Amateur Emigrant* and *Across the
   Plains.* – http://etext.library.adelaide.edu.au/

Stirling Castle: *see* Historic Scotland

Strathnaver Museum – www.strathnavermuseum.org.uk

Urquhart Castle: *see* Historic Scotland

VisitScotland – www.visitscotland.com

Ancestral Research – Government

Census information – www.scotlandspeople.gov.uk

The General Register Office website – www.gro-scotland.gov.uk

Historic Scotland – www.historic-scotland.gov.uk

National Archives (UK) – www.nationalarchives.gov.uk

National Archives of Scotland – www.nas.gov.uk

Royal Commission on the Ancient and Historical Monuments of Scotland – www.rcahms.gov.uk

Scottish Executive – www.scotland.gov.uk

Scottish Parliament – www.scottish.parliament.uk

Maps

Maps of Scotland (modern) – www.streetmap.co.uk or www.multimap.com

Map Your Ancestors – www.mapyourancestors.com

National Library of Scotland maps collection – www.nls.uk/digitallibrary/map

Ordnance Survey maps – www.old-maps.co.uk

USA

Ellis Island Museum – www.ellisisland.com

Listings of Highland games: *see* US Scots

Statue of Liberty – Ellis Island Foundation – www.ellisisland.org

Tartan Day – www.tartanday.gov.uk

Tartan Week – www.tartanweek.com

US Scots – www.usscots.com

Canada

Library and Archives Canada – www.collectionscanada.ca

Canadian Genealogy website – www.canadiangenealogy.net

Pier 21 website – www.pier21.ca

University of Guelph Scottish Studies Centre – www.uoguelph.ca/scottish

Scottish Studies Foundation – www.scottishstudies.com

New Zealand

Archives New Zealand – www.archives.govt.nz

Australia

National Library of Australia – www.nla.gov.au

National Archives of Australia – www.naa.gov.au

Ireland

Association of Professional Genealogists in Ireland – www.apgi.ie

Centre for Migration Studies (CMS) – www.qub.ac.uk/cms/

General Register Office (Northern Ireland) – www.groni.gov.uk

Hamilton and Montgomery Settlement – www.HamiltonMontgomery1606.com

North of Ireland Family History Society – www.nifhs.org

Public Record Office of Northern Ireland (PRONI) – www.proni.gov.uk

Ulster American Folk Park – www.folkpark.com

Ulster Historical Foundation, The – www.ancestryireland.com

Ulster-Scots Agency, The – www.ulsterscotsagency.com

1718 migration of Ulster-Scots – www.1718migration.org.uk

Appendix III

The 1745 Rebellion – A Touring Itinerary

THE 1745 REBELLION, often referred to simply as 'The '45', is one of the best-known episodes in Scottish history, and Prince Charles Edward Stuart (also spelled Stewart) one of the country's most iconic figures. Romantic versions of the events of 1745 and 1746 abound, and the Prince's nicknames, 'Bonnie Prince Charlie', and 'the Young Pretender', are consistent with this romantic perception. The Prince was actually born in Italy, however, to a Polish mother, and only set foot in Scotland for the first time upon arriving to begin the rebellion. His father, however, was James Francis Edward Stuart – himself the son of King James II (VII of Scotland), who was deposed in 1688 – and Charles was brought up to believe that he was the rightful heir to the Scottish throne. His arrival in Scotland in 1745 precipitated a series of battles culminating in defeat at Culloden and his subsequent flight that saw the Prince leave Scotland, never to return. Defeat at Culloden also saw the Highlands of Scotland changed forever as the Government forces wrought a brutal revenge across the area in retribution for the unsuccessful rebellion. The romance of the story aside, a Scottish monarch succeeded to the English throne in 1603 on Queen Elizabeth's death, uniting the crowns of the twin realms, and the Act of Union of the two Parliaments followed in 1707 – seen from the government's perspective, the '45 was a rebellion against the establishment.

This touring itinerary of key '45 highlights was introduced in Chapter 5 as an example of the kind of journey that can be achieved by a little research and planning. Following an itinerary of this kind enables you to construct and explore an ancestral narrative while at the same time setting it in a wider historical context. You are welcome to use this example as you wish, or to construct your own. Note, however, that you will need a car in order to follow this itinerary.

My thanks to Angela Taylor for her work on this.

The 1745 Itinerary

Spurred on by Louis xv of France and by his own father, in 1745, 25 old Charles Edward Stuart, known as Bonnie Prince Charlie, began his attempt to claim his family's right to the British crown. He hoped that with the support of both the French and his own Jacobite supporters in England, Scotland and Wales, he could overthrow the Hanoverian King, George II, and reclaim the British throne for the House of Stuart.

This itinerary follows Charles Edward Stuart's campaign journey from the raising of his standard at Glenfinnan to the sites of some of the events of the subsequent months before his defeat at Culloden Moor, which had such a devastating and lasting effect on the traditional way of life of his Highland followers. Travel through the magnificent Highlands of Scotland and experience the peace and tranquillity of the inspiring Scottish landscapes, the evocative splendour of ancient castles, the hospitality of the local people, and ultimately journey back through time to find out about the life of our ancestors over 250 years ago.

Day One

Arrive in Inverness, the beautiful, bustling capital of the Highlands. A fine introduction to the area can be found at the Inverness Museum (www.invernessmuseum.com), where the exhibitions include Jacobite memorabilia.

Inverness Castle stands nearby, though it is not as ancient a fortress as you might expect. The building you see today was built in the 1830s and is used as an administrative centre, though part of it houses an exhibition telling the story of earlier castle buildings on the site. During the 1745 rebellion, Government forces held the castle at first but it was then captured and blown up by the Jacobites.

If you want to do some ancestral research during your visit here, then a visit to the Highland Council's archive and library is a must. There is a dedicated genealogy centre where knowledgeable staff can answer queries or undertake research for you, the latter for a fee. There is more information on the Highland Council's website, www.highland.gov.uk, under the 'leisure' section heading. The Highland Family History Society has regular meetings in Inverness so you may want to check for events on their website, www.highlandfhs.org.uk.

In the evening, Eden Court Theatre www.eden-court.co.uk in Inverness is a major focus of traditional and modern cultural activity for the Highlands. You may find drama, dance, music or films to entertain you during the evening, or you can simply enjoy Inverness's variety of bars and restaurants, many of which also feature live, often traditional, music.

Day Two

Leave Inverness and take the A82 south 15 miles to Drumnadrochit. Your journey takes you along the shore of Loch Ness – keep a look out for the monster – to the splendid and atmospheric Urquhart Castle, run by Historic Scotland (www.historic-scotland.gov.uk), which stands on the shore south of Drumnadrochit. There is a visitor centre here with excellent displays depicting the history of the castle and surrounding area: it is well worth a visit.

Continue 13 miles along the shore of Loch Ness on the A82 to Invermoriston, a small hamlet on the Great Glen Way, a 73-mile hiking path that runs from Fort William to Inverness. Glenmoriston stretches out to the southwest. Take the A887 westwards through Glenmoriston then the A87 south to rejoin the A82 at Invergarry (29 miles). After the defeat at Culloden, the Prince, now a fugitive, was given shelter by outlaws known as the Seven

Men of Glenmoriston. They have an honourable place in Scottish history, having faithfully protected the Prince despite the huge bounty of £30,000 offered for his capture by the Government.

Continue southwards on the A82 for about 14 miles then take the B8004 westwards for two miles turning north, then west, on the B8005 to follow the north shore of Loch Arkaig. You will travel along the *Mile Dorch* (Dark Mile), an atmospheric route through a thickly wooded valley with mossy walls on either side. At the end of the road is a car park from where you can walk to the spectacular waterfalls of Eas Chia-aig. The loch is the fabled hiding place of French gold that was on its way to the aid of Jacobites in 1746. No one has ever found the gold, so presumably it still lies hidden nearby.

Retrace your route back via the B8005 and B8004 towards the A82. Now travel southwards via the A82 to Fort William, the largest town in the West Highlands and a popular tourist destination. It nestles next to Loch Linnhe at the foot of Ben Nevis, Britain's highest mountain, which towers impressively over the town. The Gaelic name for Fort William, *An Gearasdan* (literally 'the garrison'), refers to the fort that was built by the government there to control the area following Cromwell's invasion during the English Civil War. You can still visit the ruins of the fort along the seafront wall in the centre of town.

Day Three

Today, take the A82 north from Fort William and, after a mile and a half, turn west on to the A830 which runs 17 miles along the north shore of Loch Eil to Glenfinnan. It was here that Bonnie Prince Charlie landed in Scotland and started to gather together his Highland army in August 1745. He raised his standard and addressed the 2,500 men who had gathered to support his cause, mainly members of the MacDonald, Cameron and Macdonnell clans. It is said that some of the clan leaders urged the Prince to abandon his scheme, but despite his refusal to heed their advice they remained loyal and followed him. The Glenfinnan Monument located here is a tribute to the men who fought and died for the Prince. You can find out more at the Glenfinnan Visitor Centre, run by the National Trust for Scotland (www.nts.org.uk).

Continue west on the A830 for 13 miles, and just past Kinlochnanuagh, on the shore of Loch nan Uamh, you will find Prince Charlie's Cairn, a mound of stones marking the end of his year long campaign, where the fugitive prince was finally rescued by a French frigate and made his escape to France.

Drive eastwards on the A830 back to Fort William where you turn south on the A82 which turns east at Ballachulish to take you through the magnificent scenery of Glen Coe (17 miles) and the Loch Lomond and the Trossachs National Park. At Crianlarich (36 miles) leave the A82 and head east then south on the A85. After 16 miles, at Lochearnhead, continue southwards on the A84 for 32 miles. This route takes you to the historic city of Stirling.

Day Four

Stirling surrendered to the Prince and his Jacobite forces in January of 1746. It is an attractive city overlooked by the impressive Stirling Castle, run by Historic Scotland, which towers above the river and the site of the medieval bridge so important to William Wallace in earlier Scottish history. The castle was a favoured retreat of the Stuart monarchs and the childhood home of Mary Queen of Scots, and is undergoing impressive restoration.

Fifteen miles or so southeast of Stirling via the A9, you will find Falkirk. An obelisk on the southwest edge of the town marks the site of the Battle of Falkirk Muir, where on 17 January 1746 the Prince and his Jacobite army were victorious against the Government troops. Whilst in Falkirk you can visit Callendar House Museum (www.falkirk.gov.uk/cultural/museums/museums.htm) where exhibitions take you through local history from the Jacobite uprisings to the industrial revolution.

Now, head on to Edinburgh (just 25 miles from Falkirk) along the A9 and then the M9 motorway, and arrive in Scotland's magnificent historic capital. The M9 takes you close to Edinburgh airport from where the A8 runs eastwards into the heart of the city.

Charles Edward Stuart started his campaign by taking Perth in early September 1745, followed by the unopposed capitulation of Edinburgh on 16 September.

Day Five

There are many things to do and places to visit in Edinburgh. A good starting point is the Museum of Scotland (www.nms.ac.uk) in Chambers Street. Here, you will find artefacts from the history of Scotland, from early geological times through to the present day. At the nearby Scottish Genealogical Society library and study centre, (www.scotsgenealogy.com) you'll find plenty of fellow travellers and enthusiastic researchers, as well as a wealth of genealogical information and guidance.

A must-see place in Edinburgh in relation to Bonnie Prince Charlie is the Palace of Holyroodhouse at the end of Edinburgh's historic Royal Mile. The Palace is where the Prince stayed during his time in Edinburgh, and is still in use as a residence by the current Royal Family during their visits to the city. The new Scottish Parliament lies very nearby. Access to the impressive and controversial building is free and guided tours are available at a charge. At the other end of the Royal Mile is Edinburgh Castle, (www. historic-scotland.gov.uk) from the battlements of which you can enjoy commanding views out over both the New and Old Towns of Edinburgh.

A few days after capturing Edinburgh, the Prince took his Jacobite army to fight against government forces camped at Prestonpans a few miles to the east of the city. Take the A1 eastwards from Edinburgh, joining local roads at Meadowmill. You can walk the battlefield at Prestonpans with the help of a printed guide, which you can download from the Prestoungrange

Gothenburg visitor centre website (www.prestoungrange.org) or visit the centre in person to pick up the leaflet.

After his victory at Prestonpans, Prince Charles was determined to march into England despite the contrary advice of a number of his Scottish supporters. Advancing with his army, he made it as far south as Derby, and then hesitated as he awaited support from both France and his English and Welsh supporters. When these did not appear, he returned to Scotland, but was now closely pursued by government troops led by the Duke of Cumberland.

Day Six

Travel west via the A8 out of Edinburgh and then northwards on the M9 and A9 to make your way to Kingussie and Newtonmore (about 120 miles from Edinburgh). Here you will find two fascinating Highland Folk Museums (www.highlandfolk.com) at which more than 400 years of Highland history are brought to life in exhibitions that track the everyday experiences of clansman and crofter. The 1700s Highland township that has been reconstructed based on archaeological evidence is of particular interest. *Baile Gean*, or the Township of Goodwill, as it is known, is a fascinating insight into ordinary life at the time.

Just south of Kingussie are Ruthven Barracks (www.historic-scotland.gov.uk) perched on top of a steep glacial mound with views of the surrounding mountains and glens. This was one of four fortified barracks built by the government to control the Highland people after the failed 1715 Jacobite uprising. After their defeat at Culloden in the 1745 rebellion, the remaining Jacobite soldiers regrouped at Ruthven and awaited the Prince there to continue the campaign. Charles, however, had by this time given up hope and only wanted to flee from the Duke of Cumberland to safety. He sent word that each man should save himself, and in this way the uprising ended. The remaining Jacobite men burned the barracks and all that remains here today is as it was left by the Jacobites.

After your visit to the barracks, rejoin the A9 and continue north for 42 miles to Inverness to spend the evening relaxing in advance of tomorrow, what will be an important day for you.

Day Seven

On the last day of your tour, make the short journey east to Culloden via the A96 where, on 16 April 1746, Bonnie Prince Charlie's Jacobite dream was shattered by Government forces. Both sides were supported by different clansmen, but the Duke of Cumberland's professional army hugely outnumbered the Prince's dispirited force. The bloody battle only lasted an hour, but was followed by a massacre of the Highland forces, and later by years of reprisals and the suppression of the Highland clans.

In a timely and important project, the Culloden Visitor Centre is being redesigned by the National Trust for Scotland (www.nts.org.uk) and the battlefield is being restored to the way it was on the eve of the battle. A reinterpretation of the battlefield will help you understand the events that took place here, and this will be perhaps the most moving and powerful experience of your journey: here, you truly touch the past and its effect on history. For more information about this important project visit www.culloden.org.uk

Day Eight

Depart Inverness, taking with you the memories of Scotland's story, and your own. I hope you have enjoyed the journey, and that is has given you deeper insight into Scotland's past, and through this, your own.

Some other books published by **LUATH** PRESS

Scottish Roots: step-by-step guide for ancestor hunters

Alwyn James
ISBN 1 84282 090 7 PBK £6.99

Who? When? Where? Alwyn James's revised guide to genealogy provides the answers.

Clear step-by-step instructions and useful advice for tracing your family tree.

The ideal starting point even for those who knew little more than a grandparent.

No need to be on the spot – includes a chapter on distance research.

How to start, all the preparations required. For anyone interested in researching their family history, *Scottish Roots* provides an excellent, comprehensible step-by-step guide to tracing your Scottish ancestry. Using the example of two Scots trying to discover their roots, Alwyn James illustrates how easy it is to commence the research process and gradually compile a worthwhile family tree. He navigates the reader through the first steps of sourcing family details, making contact with distant relatives and preparing to collate any new information.

Now in its 20th year of publication, this new and updated edition of the guide includes information on how to access family data utilising electronic resources and the Internet – a must if conducting research from an overseas base. A very welcome addition to the family library.

Wherever the Saltire Flies

Kenny MacAskill and Henry McLeish
ISBN 1 905222 68 8 PBK £8.99

For Scots living in Scotland today, the idea of a society of exiled and ancestral Scots in another country conjures up varying images of nostalgia and sentimentality for their homeland.

For emigrant and ancestral Scots around the world, Scottish societies offer a chance for like-minded, passionate people to join together in celebrating past and contemporary Scotland.

Based on a series of lively interviews with members of Scottish societies, *Wherever the Saltire Flies* charts a memorable journey in the ever-evolving concept of Scottish identity. Providing genuine support and inspiration, these societies play a huge part in the preservation of Scottish culture and the worldwide promotion of Scotland, and the people involved are as much a part of Scottish history as those living in Scotland.

Global Scots: Voices from Afar

Kenny MacAskill and Henry McLeish
ISBN 1 905222 37 8 PBK £9.99

Why leave Scotland? What has Scotland provided? What has Scotland failed to provide? What does it mean to be Scottish elsewhere in the world?

Global Scots is a series of over 30 interviews with highly successful expatriate Scots around the world. The interviewees, all of whom grew up in Scotland – including iconic photographer Harry Benson; Chairman of Walt Disney Consumer Products, Andy Mooney; and comedian/presenter Craig Ferguson – reflect on issues such as identity, sectarianism and dour Scottish Sundays.

Although the interviewees vary in age, background and profession, certain values and feelings are universal. They all remain committed to the land they were brought up in, remaining distinctively Scottish no matter where they are in the world, be it Toronto or Tallinn.

These voices from afar provide valuable insights into Scotland's role in the modern world. Reflective and often hard-hitting, the perspectives they offer on their native country are enlightening, entertaining and potentially beneficial to a new devolved Scotland.

Scots in Canada

Jenni Calder
ISBN 1 84282 038 9 PBK £7.99

The story of the Scots who went to Canada, from the 17th century onwards.

In Canada there are nearly as many descendants of Scots as there are people living in Scotland; almost five million Canadians ticked the 'Scottish origin' box in the most recent Canadian Census. Many Scottish families have friends or relatives in Canada.

Thousands of Scots were forced from their homeland, while others chose to leave, seeking a better life. As individuals, families and communities, they braved the wild Atlantic ocean, many crossing in cramped under-rationed ships, unprepared for the fierce Canadian winter. And yet Scots went on to lay railroads, found banks and exploit the fur trade, and helped form the political infrastructure of modern day Canada.

Meticulously researched and fluently written... it neatly charts the rise of a country without succumbing to sentimental myths.
SCOTLAND ON SUNDAY

Calder celebrates the ties that still bind Canada and Scotland in camaraderie after nearly 400 years of relations.
THE CHRONICLE HERALD, NOVA SCOTIA

On the Trail of Bonnie Prince Charlie

David R. Ross
ISBN 0 946487 68 5 PBK £7.99

On the Trail of Bonnie Prince Charlie is the story of the Young Pretender. Born in Italy, grandson of James VII, at a time when the German house of Hanover was on the throne, his father was regarded by many as the rightful king. Bonnie Prince Charlie's campaign to retake the throne in his father's name changed the fate of Scotland. The Jacobite movement was responsible for the '45 Uprising, one of the most decisive times in Scottish history. The suffering following the battle of Culloden in 1746 still evokes emotion. Charles' own journey immediately after Culloden is well known: hiding in the heather, escaping to Skye with Flora MacDonald. Little is known of his return to London in 1750 incognito, where he converted to Protestantism (he reconverted to Catholicism before he died and is buried in the Vatican).

- 79 places to visit in Scotland and England
- One general map and 4 location maps
- Prestonpans, Clifton, Falkirk and Culloden
- Battle plans
- Simplified family tree
- Rarely seen illustrations

Knowing the story behind the place can bring the landscape to life. Take this book with you on your travels and follow the route taken by Charles' forces on their doomed march.

Ross writes with an immediacy, a dynamism, that makes his subjects come alive on the page.
DUNDEE COURIER

The Quest for the Celtic Key

Karen Ralls-MacLeod and Ian Robertson
ISBN 1 84282 031 1 PBK £8.99

Full of mystery, magic and intrigue, Scotland's past is still burning with unanswered questions. Many of these have been asked before, some have never before been broached – but all are addressed with the inquisitiveness of true detectives in *The Quest for the Celtic Key*.

Who was the 'Wizard of the North'?
Was Winston Churchill really a practising member of a Druid order?
What are the similarities between Merlin and Christ?
Did Arthur, king of the Britons, conquer Scotland and was he buried in Govan?

Encompassing well-known events and personae – such as Robert the Bruce, William Wallace, the Declaration of Arbroath and the Stone of Destiny – whilst also tackling the more obscure elements in Scottish history – the significance of the number 19, the power of the colour green and the spiritual meaning of locations across Scotland – *The Quest for the Celtic Key* illustrates how the seemingly disparate 'mysteries of history' are connected.

A travelogue which enriches the mythologies and histories so beautifully told, with many newly wrought connection to places, buildings stones and other remains.
REV. DR MICHAEL NORTHCOTT, Faculty of Divinity, University of Edinburgh

Scots in the USA

Jenni Calder

ISBN 1 905222 06 8 PBK £8.99

The map of the United States is peppered with Scottish place-names and America's telephone directories are filled with surnames illustrating Scottish ancestry. Increasingly, Americans of Scottish extraction are visiting Scotland in search of their family history. All over Scotland and the United States there are clues to the Scottish-American relationship, the legacy of centuries of trade and communication as well as that of departure and heritage.

The experiences of Scottish settlers in the United States varied enormously, as did their attitudes to the lifestyles that they left behind and those that they began anew once they arrived in North America.

Scots in the USA discusses why they left Scotland, where they went once they reached the United States, and what they did when they got there.

. . . a valuable readable and illuminating addition to a burgeoning literature. . . should be required reading on the flight to New York by all those on the Tartan Week trail.

Alan Taylor, SUNDAY HERALD

The Ultimate Burns Supper Book

Clark McGinn

ISBN 1 905222 60 2 PBK £7.99

Everything you need to enjoy or arrange a Burns Supper – just add food, drink and friends.

Clark McGinn, one of the foremost Burns Supper speakers in the world, presents *The Ultimate Burns Supper Book*. Containing all the information you need to enjoy a Supper, whether as host, speaker or guest, this book is full of advice, anecdotes, poetry and wit.

Includes:

A complete run through of what to expect on the night, with a list of courses and speeches

Advice on what to wear

A section on how to prepare and present speeches

A list of common Burns Supper questions (and their answers!)

A selection of Burns's greatest poems, including a full English verse translation of the 'Address to a Haggis'

Answers your concerns about eating haggis and extols the pleasures of drinking whisky

HISTORY

For Freedom: the last days of William Wallace
David R. Ross
ISBN 1 905222 28 9 PBK £9.99

Desire Lines: A Scottish Odyssey
David R. Ross
ISBN 1 84282 033 8 PBK £9.99

A Passion for Scotland
David R. Ross
ISBN 1 84282 019 2 PBK £5.99

Blind Harry's Wallace
William Hamilton of Gilbert
ISBN 0 946487 33 2 PBK £8.99

Braveheart: From Hollywood to Holyrood
Lin Anderson
ISBN 1 84282 066 4 PBK £7.99

The Highland Clearances Trail
Rob Gibson
ISBN 1 905222 10 6 PBK £5.99

Scotch on the Rocks
Arthur Swinson
ISBN 1 905222 09 2 PBK £7.99

LANGUAGE

Luath Scots Language Learner
L Colin Wilson
ISBN 0 946487 91 X PBK £9.99
ISBN 1 84282 026 5 CD £16.99

FOLKLORE

Luath Storyteller: Tales of the Picts
Stuart McHardy
ISBN 1 84282 097 4 PBK £5.99

Luath Storyteller: Highland Myths & Legends
George W Macpherson
ISBN 1 84282 064 8 PBK £5.99

The Supernatural Highlands
Francis Thompson
ISBN 0 946487 31 6 PBK £8.99

ON THE TRAIL OF

On the Trail of the Holy Grail
Stuart McHardy
ISBN 1 905222 53 X PBK £7.99

On the Trail of Scotland's Myths and Legends
Stuart McHardy
ISBN 1 84282 049 4 PBK £7.99

THE QUEST FOR

The Quest for the Wicker Man
ed. Benjamin Franks et al
ISBN 1 905222 18 1 HBK £16.99

The Quest for Charles Rennie Mackintosh
John Cairney
ISBN 1 84282 058 3 HBK £16.99

ISLANDS

Lewis & Harris: History & Pre-History
Francis Thompson
ISBN 0 946487 77 4 PBK £4.99

FICTION

Writing in the Sand
Angus Dunn
ISBN 1 905222 47 5 PBK £12.99

Heartland
John MacKay
ISBN 1 905222 11 4 PBK £6.99

Last of the Line
John MacKay
ISBN 1 905222 55 6 PBK £9.99

Luath Press Limited
committed to publishing well written books worth reading

LUATH PRESS takes its name from Robert Burns, whose little collie Luath (*Gael.*, swift or nimble) tripped up Jean Armour at a wedding and gave him the chance to speak to the woman who was to be his wife and the abiding love of his life. Burns called one of 'The Twa Dogs' Luath after Cuchullin's hunting dog in *Ossian's Fingal*. Luath Press was established in 1981 in the heart of Burns country, and now resides a few steps up the road from Burns' first lodgings on Edinburgh's Royal Mile.

Luath offers you distinctive writing with a hint of unexpected pleasures.

Most bookshops in the UK, the US, Canada, Australia, New Zealand and parts of Europe either carry our books in stock or can order them for you. To order direct from us, please send a £sterling cheque, postal order, international money order or your credit card details (number, address of cardholder and expiry date) to us at the address below. Please add post and packing as follows: UK – £1.00 per delivery address; overseas surface mail – £2.50 per delivery address; overseas airmail – £3.50 for the first book to each delivery address, plus £1.00 for each additional book by airmail to the same address. If your order is a gift, we will happily enclose your card or message at no extra charge.

Luath Press Limited
543/2 Castlehill
The Royal Mile
Edinburgh EH1 2ND
Scotland
Telephone: 0131 225 4326 (24 hours)
Fax: 0131 225 4324
email: sales@luath.co.uk
Website: www.luath.co.uk